Raising Ethical Children

10 Keys to Helping Your Children Become Moral and Caring

Steven Carr Reuben, Ph.D.

Prima Publishing
P.O. Box 1260BK
Rocklin, CA 95677
(916) 786-0426

Production by Robin Lockwood, Bookman Productions
Copyediting by Lura Harrison
Typography by Bookman Productions
Interior design by Robin Lockwood
Cover design by The Dunlavey Studio, Sacramento
Cover photo © Sharpshooters/Jeff Turnau

Library of Congress Cataloging-in-Publication Data

Reuben, Steven Carr.
    Raising ethical children : 10 keys to helping your children become moral and caring/by Steven Carr Reuben.
      p. cm.
    Includes index.
    ISBN 1-55958-360-6
    1. Moral development.   2. Moral education.
    3. Child rearing.
I. Title
BF723.M54R49   1993   93-17736
649'.7—dc20   CIP

94 95 96 97 98 RRD 10 9 8 7 6 5 4 3 2 1
Printed in the United States of America

How to Order:

Single copies may be ordered from Prima Publishing, P.O. Box 1260BK, Rocklin, CA 95677; telephone (916) 786-0426. Quantity discounts are also available. On your letterhead, include information regarding the intended use of the books and the number of books you wish to purchase.

This book is dedicated to my stepdaughter Gable. She has taught me more about ethical parenting than all the books I have ever read, and given me more joy, satisfaction, and fulfillment in my life than I could ever have thought possible. If all children had her kindness, her caring, her sense of empathy for all creatures large and small, and that special sweetness in her soul, the world would be a wonderful place indeed.

Acknowledgments

As always, I cannot adequately reflect in words the debt I owe my wife and life partner, Didi, for her constant inspiration, support, feedback, suggestions, and for role modeling each day what it truly means to be an ethical human being.

I will always be grateful for the lifelong influence of my parents, Dr. Jack and Betty Reuben. No child could ask for more outstanding moral role models. I would feel immensely successful as a parent if I could live up to the examples that they have always set for me.

Thanks to Leslie Parness, my agent, for her constant enthusiasm for my work and encouragement of my writing, and for consistently believing that what I have to say would be of value to others.

Of course I owe a great debt of thanks to all the wonderful people at Prima Publishing—to Ben Dominitz, Jennifer Basye, Andi Reese Brady, and the rest of the Prima extended family—for having faith enough in my writing to share it with the world, and to Robin Lockwood and Bookman Productions for creating such a beautiful book.

Contents

Contents

Introduction

As a tiny child I turned from the window
out of which I was watching a snowstorm, and
hopefully asked, "Mama, do we believe in Winter?"

—Philip Roth

One of the most riveting pictures of the Los Angeles civil disturbances of May 1992 was the image captured on live television of a mother with young children in hand, walking into a store to participate in the looting. As I joined millions of other viewers in witnessing this scene, I was painfully aware of the undisputed truth that, more powerfully than the words of any book, sermon, or lesson in school, children learn ethics and values primarily from what they live each day.

During those dark and painful days as this mother/child looting scene was repeated hundreds of times, I couldn't help but wonder about the lifelong lessons that these children were learning in that indelibly etched environment.

How do our children learn right from wrong? How do we teach them to be the kind of people who enhance rather than diminish the quality of life on our planet? How do we pass on to them a sense of morality, values, and social responsibility, which is so crucial for the fundamental decency needed for our society to endure? Are there easily understood keys to raising ethical children that can be incorporated into our everyday parenting? These are some of the questions that will be raised and answered in this book.

I am convinced that parents do want their children to be moral, caring, ethical human beings. They want them to grow up with strong, positive self-images and an inner certainty that who they are matters, what they do matters, how they talk matters, what they make of their lives matters, and the kind of people they become matters.

Through the pages of *Raising Ethical Children*, you will: meet child development experts who have studied moral development in children; learn about the best current thinking on establishing guidelines for discipline at home; find ways to encourage ethical decision making in your children; learn to cope with the pressures of peers and friendships; and learn the incredible power of positive self-esteem and the importance of teaching your child that there is fundamental value and meaning to life.

In addition, we will explore together the process of making ethical choices and working with your children to create an ethical vision for their lives. You will learn about the importance of becoming a moral model for your children and how to use the ancient wisdom of Western religious traditions, which stretch back thousands of years and are rooted in the fundamental moral principles that have successfully withstood the test of time.

The purpose of this book is to help parents identify in a simple, accessible, concrete fashion those actions which can help children make ethical connections in their lives. Throughout the book there are numerous specific techniques for working with your own family that will give you simple parenting tools for encouraging ethical behavior.

As a rabbi working in the field of spiritual and moral education for over twenty years, I have come to have a great appreciation for the importance of developing mentor models in the area of ethical training and moral education. Our everyday lives are literally filled with positive examples of good ethical behavior that mostly go unrecognized and unacknowledged. What this means is that most of the time we fail to exploit the powerful educational potential of these daily moral models, even though they can easily provide inspiration, education, and motivation for our children if utilized properly.

While I was in the midst of writing this book, my six-year-old niece went to the store in the hopes of buying a gerbil as a pet. The wise owner of the pet store told her, "First pick it up and hold it. If you can't pick it up and cuddle with it, then you aren't ready to take one home as a pet."

When I heard the story I kept thinking, "How come no one ever asks the same of potential parents, before they are allowed to take kids home?" Every child deserves unconditional love, affection, attention, and positive reinforcement so that they will develop a strong sense of positive self-esteem. Only then will they see other human beings as worthy of their care, of their love, and of being treated ethically.

A story of moral habits: While on a family driving trip to the Grand Canyon a couple of summers ago, we stopped at a small town restaurant in Williams, Arizona. At a table nearby, a young man of about seven was waiting with great impatience for his food to arrive (the service was incredibly slow!). He was obviously very hungry and irritable, and it was all he could do to stay in his chair while eagerly waiting for that hamburger and french fries to arrive.

After what seemed to be an interminable wait, when his food was finally placed in front of him, I watched in fascination as he first began to reach for the hamburger, then caught himself in mid-reach, folded his hands tightly, closed his eyes, and obviously uttered a fast silent "grace" over his food. Then his eyes popped open with relief, and he dove into that hamburger and french fries with delight.

Watching that young boy's automatic, well-trained moral habit of prayer, as well as his recognition that he had a moral obligation to be thankful for his food, brought home a simple but significant lesson about the power of developing moral habits in the everyday lives of our children.

This book can serve as both a source for understanding the important ethical and moral values rooted in ancient traditions of the past that you wish to pass on to your children and as an inspirational look at how others have transformed those everyday "teachable moments" of moral mentoring into powerful lessons for their daily lives.

I am eager to hear of your own successes in transmitting ethical values to your children, and welcome any suggestions, reactions, ideas, or personal stories that I might share with others in the future. I can be reached at Kehillath Israel, 16019 Sunset Blvd., Pacific Palisades, California, 90272.

One

The Challenge of Raising Ethical Children

From the day your child is born you must teach him to do things. Children today love luxury too much. They have detestable manners, flout authority, have no respect for their elders. They no longer rise when their parents and teachers enter the room. What kind of awful creatures will they be when they grow up?

Socrates, 399 B.C.E.

Throughout the nearly twenty years of my work with parents and children of all ages, repeatedly I have been asked questions like these: "How do you teach ethics to a child? What suggestions can you offer that will help me guide my child to making the right choices and decisions in life? What hints might you offer me to encourage my children to be more ethical, caring, compassionate human beings?"

Parents are constantly searching for concrete, easily understandable suggestions and guidelines that will give specific ideas to encourage value-centered parenting. That is precisely what this book is about. I hope the many specific suggestions and ideas that are shared within these pages will provide both concrete help and realistic guidelines that parents will find truly useful in their search for the keys to raising children in this contemporary world.

The first important step is to ask yourself what your *goals* are as a parent. What do you want to accomplish with your children? What kind of people do you want them to grow up to be? How do you want them to relate to others? What are the characteristics and qualities you most want to nurture and develop in them? The clearer you are about these dreams and goals, the easier it is to focus on the appropriate strategies and methods for achieving them.

The truth is, most of us will continue to ask ourselves throughout our children's lives what kind of human beings we hope they will be. We imagine the kinds of behavior they would have to exhibit for us to feel we are successful parents and to see them as successful, competent, caring, and ethical human beings.

Ethical Expectations

Perhaps one of our most important goals ought to be to instill in our children "ethical expectations" of their own behavior—that still, small inner voice that whispers, *"I can make a difference. What I do matters. What I say matters. Who I am matters.*" When ethical expectations are solidly integrated into their understanding of self, children more easily become ethically self-regulating and ethically self-motivated.

"Ethically self-regulating" children are those who, in essence, carry around their own *internal* voice of conscience. This internal voice is constantly giving feedback to the moral centers of these children's psyches, letting them know whether or not a particular behavior they are contemplating is consistent with their own internalized ethical code.

"Ethically self-motivated" children are children whose natural inclination is to treat other human beings in ways that are acceptable and desirable in society. One of the primary ways that children learn to become ethically self-motivated is by living in a family environment enriched with opportunities for positive ethical decision making. In such an environment their experiences with making ethical decisions will produce positive, nurturing, ego-supporting feedback from adults that they respect, admire, and love.

Parenting in Uncharted Waters

The world in which our children are growing up is increasingly complex, and confusing for parents of all ages. All of us are constantly bombarded with a dizzying array of values and ethical decisions, from television, radio, and the movies; religious institutions and political leaders; and friends and family. The choices we make as parents, and the choices our children are confronted with today, seem much more serious, much more life-threatening and significant than they ever did in ages past.

Gone is the "Father Knows Best" fantasy of the perfect family, with children whose greatest ethical choices were whether or not to tell mom they broke a vase while playing catch in the house. As shocking as it seems, the U.S. Census Bureau reported in 1991 that only 1.6 percent of families in America now fit the traditional stereotypical image of a breadwinning father and a mother who stays at home with the kids.

In many ways, parenting today takes a tremendous amount of courage. It is a leap of faith into the unknown. It requires courage to cast about in uncharted waters. As one parent once beautifully put it, "Deciding to have a child is to make the momentous decision to have your heart walk around outside your body for the rest of your life."

As parents today, we face challenges that were simply unheard of a generation or two ago. In the same way, our children's lives are radically different from those of the past. In fact, one of the things that makes parenting today so frightening is that the vast array of challenges and fears our children face daily are of an entirely different nature than ever before.

Just look at the startling comparison between the top seven problems reported by schools in 1940 and those in 1987. In 1940, the most important school problems included talking out of turn, chewing gum, making noise, running in the halls, cutting in line, dress code infractions, and loitering. Such benign behavior has been so transformed by the realities of our modern era that by 1987 the top school problems were drug abuse, alcohol abuse, pregnancy, suicide, rape, robbery, and assault!

We can't help but shake our heads in disbelief at the often terrifying world in which our children live. Where can they go for a sense of security, safety, and refuge from the stresses and strains of daily life? How can we make our homes sanctuaries of security, havens of love and acceptance, safe harbors of emotional support and physical shelter from the storms of the outside world?

Problems are not only found in the halls of our educational institutions. They are also found in the general social environment that surrounds us. Witness the culture of conspicuous consumerism, the almost universal breakdown of traditional family values, and the ever-increasing rate of divorce that has produced a wider range of nontraditional family structures and configurations than ever before in human history. All these forces have an impact on the lives of our children and reflect the general social environment in which we make our parenting choices and ethical decisions.

Raising ethical children is a great and noble challenge. As difficult as it may seem, it is one of the most important tasks we will ever have. In fact, you might cogently argue that the entire fate of the world and the future of humanity are dependent upon whether, as a whole, we are successful in bringing up children who will help the world become a sanctuary of wholeness, a source of caring and compassion, and a home of healing for all who suffer from wants of body or spirit. Simply put, the kind of children we raise will determine the kind of world in which they will live.

Meeting Basic Emotional Needs First

Before you can begin to instill an understanding of and an appreciation for the interrelatedness of all human beings, before you can train your children in the art of making ethical decisions, you must first fulfill their most basic emotional and psychological needs. No child can attend to the realm of the ethical before his or her fundamental emotional and psychological needs are met. These are needs for belonging, for feeling important, for feeling that who they are matters, for feeling self-worth, for feeling loved and accepted—and after basic physical needs are met, they take precedence over *everything else in the child's life.* That is precisely why it is so crucial for parents to ensure that these most basic emotional needs are met first. Only then will children have the emotional strength and stability to move to the next level and reach out to the emotional world beyond the self.

This need for attending to the underlying psychology of children reminds me of something that Gandhi once said in reflecting upon the state of the people in his country, India. A commentator was castigating the ordinary Indians on the street for not being more "religious," and specifically for not being more "Christian." Gandhi's response was a sad shake of his head and the comment, "My people are so poor, that God can only appear to them in the form of a piece of bread." Gandhi recognized that until the most basic physical and emotional needs were met, there was little room for the higher issues of morality, ethics, and the struggle to discover meaning and purpose in life. The same is true when it comes to your children and their emotional needs.

Later in this book, I will discuss the importance of self-esteem, and my conviction that nurturing feelings of self-worth in your children is the single most important gift that you can ever give them. I truly believe it is more important than material wealth, more important than toys or games, computers or large-screen TVs, their first automobile, a new dress for Confirmation, or even having two parents living at home with them. The ability to feel that they are *worthy* of being loved, *worthy* of being cared for, *worthy* of parents who spend one-on-one time with them, *worthy* of being treated with dignity and respect—these are the gifts that form the very heart of their self-image, and as such, the source of their ability to empathize with and care about other human beings as well.

Treat Your Children Ethically

After establishing a firm foundation of self-respect and self-worth, the first key to raising ethical children is to *treat your children ethically*. You must create an ethical environment in which your children grow, mature, and come to understand ethical behavior, through the experience of living in the kind of family that embodies in its everyday activities those same ethical standards that are ultimately expected of them as well. This is the first great challenge of raising ethical children, and it requires an ethical consciousness that pervades every aspect of our parenting lives.

Teachable Moments

The great Australian educator Sylvia Ashton Warner coined the term "teachable moments" to refer to all those unpredictable times during student–teacher interactions in which the child is suddenly open, eager, reachable—teachable. The challenge for teachers is to create an environment that stimulates and encourages positive teachable moments for their students, and to act each day knowing that *every* action might be the one that these students choose to emulate.

The same holds true for parents. Since we never really can know in advance which of the thousands of moments we spend with our children will turn out to be one of those memorable teachable moments, the challenge is to act *always* in ways that we would be proud to have our children emulate. Only then will we feel secure that whatever behavior of ours our children choose to copy will result in the kind of ethical behavior that we wish to teach them in the first place.

Look back at your own childhood. Could the moments that had a significant impact on your ethical development have been predicted in advance? Likewise, the powerful, important moments that happen between us and our children simply can't be scheduled. They most often arise spontaneously—perhaps a casual encounter with a homeless woman on the street where our children witness a situation that calls for an ethical decision.

You can't simply schedule "quality time" to discuss ethics or morality. It doesn't work to write in next week's daily calendar, "Teach Susan how to be an ethical person next Sunday, from 3–4 P.M." Accept that your children's real lessons come from being with, living with, and interacting with you day in and day out in a hundred different ways that you can never identify or predict in advance.

Perhaps the best that you can do is to be clear about the values you want to teach, ensure that the way you live your own life is consistent with those values, and be the kind of adult you want your children to grow up to be. Life is learned from living with people, just as loving is learned from being loved first by parents, then by extended family, and eventually by ourselves.

Your children learn ethics primarily through their interactions with family, friends, and community. They can only truly learn what it means to be ethical, responsible human beings by living in the context of a larger community. The sensitivity to others' needs that marks an ethical person develops primarily from ethical interaction with others—interaction that demonstrates mutual respect, a sense of justice and fairness, and an understanding of our interdependence upon one another.

There is a famous story in Jewish tradition of two men adrift in a rowboat in the middle of the ocean. As the story goes, all at once one of the men took out a hand drill and began to drill a hole in the bottom of the boat. His partner,

upon seeing what was going on, shouted with justifiable
alarm, "Are you crazy? What are you doing? You'll sink the
boat!" At that point the man with the drill calmly replied,
"What are you getting upset about? After all, I'm only
drilling under *my* seat!" You see, no matter what we do,
there is just no way to avoid the responsibility of being
interconnected with every other human being on earth,
and the lessons we must teach our children in order for our
planet to survive all rest upon this profound and essential
supposition.

The "Internal Parent"

One of the most important challenges that parents face in
raising ethical children is instilling in them what I like to
call the "internal parent." Like the role that Jiminy Cricket
played in *Pinocchio,* the internal parent is the still small
voice of conscience that whispers "yes" or "no" whenever
we are confronted with ethical choices and dilemmas. Our
job as parents is to provide our children with enough
hands-on personal experiences that they have a substantial
ethical memory bank from which they can draw whenever
the need arises. These experiences can be examples from
our own lives, lessons from the lives of others, or moral
guidelines (often in the form of easy-to-remember ethical
mottoes, sayings, or phrases).

   The primary model for our children's growing sense of
what is right and wrong behavior is naturally found within
their family. Children watch, learn, and then imitate in one
form or another choices, actions, and decisions they see
their parents or siblings make. It is from watching their
family that children form their sense of values and learn
important behavior patterns that will subsequently guide
the rest of their lives.

Within the primary family unit children discover what is expected of each individual, all of whom have slightly different places and roles within the family system. Here children learn what is expected of a mother or a father, of a brother or a sister, how a father or mother is supposed to treat his or her spouse and children, which behavior is acceptable and which unacceptable, and which you keep a secret and which you talk about openly. In short, children absorb, learn, and then emulate literally thousands of bits of information on how families work and what the role of each individual is within the family. Then they use that information, day after day, year after year.

Standing Up for Your Own Values

Your children *need* you to stand for something. They need you to have clear ethical standards and values. Above all, they need you to articulate those values verbally and through your own actions. Ideally, you will consistently reinforce your ethical guidelines as part of a parenting team that nurtures self-worth and emotional security and helps them make sense out of the seemingly unethical world that surrounds them.

Creating such a value-centered home is, of course, not dependent on the number of parents in attendance, or even the kind of family structure that may exist. Whether you are married or single, gay or straight, raising your children alone or in a shared living arrangement, the essential core of your children's values must be both clearly spelled out and *lived out* within their home environment.

If we are honest with ourselves, we will admit that all values are *not* equal in our eyes, and although we may defend the rights of anyone to believe whatever they choose, we also believe they must take responsibility for the results of those values as they are manifested through actions that affect the lives of others. In truth most of us are not willing to leave the arena of ethics and values to the pure "I'm OK, you're OK" crowd, for we realize that to do so is essentially to abdicate our moral responsibility for establishing ethical guidelines for ourselves and our children. In such a "values-neutral" world, one could logically argue that even Nazis would have the right to assert that their ethical beliefs are as valid as anyone else's! Yet, the entire world has already learned the painful lesson that such a policy of ethical neutrality leads to action that causes untold pain, suffering, and oppression to others. Unfortunately, this is the logical result of all values being equal and of parents embracing the goal of simply allowing each person to "clarify" his or her own beliefs, regardless of whether or not they are truly ethical.

If you embrace all values in general, in the end you are left embracing no values in particular. Thus if you embrace all values (even if sincerely held and passionately espoused) as being equally valid, you are not only undermining the very moral and ethical foundation of Western society but sowing the seeds of moral indecision in your children as well.

Raising ethical children is the result of consistently communicating in every way you can the solid, identifiable, living ethical values that underlie your interactions with the world in every area of your life, both personal and professional. Whether at home, at work, with friends in social settings, at sporting events, in social and service clubs or community activities, perhaps the single most important thing you can do for your children is to make sure that they see you "walk your talk." Obviously, if you espouse one set of values at home and interact with the world in a way that belies those values, your children will learn that ethics and values are merely slogans to be mouthed, and that what is really expected of them is to be hypocritical—to say one thing and do another.

I know the most powerful lessons I learned from my parents took place from simply watching them live their lives consistently in accordance with the values they taught. Going with my mother to walk precincts to support candidates in whom she believed. Traveling at age twelve with my father on a Boy Scout trip whose purpose was to bring clothes and toys to impoverished youth in Mexico. Watching them support with their time as well as their money the causes, organizations, and individuals who worked to bring greater dignity, self-worth, health, and education to children and parents who suffered from abuse and the neglect of poverty. All were powerful lessons to me about my responsibility as a human being to act in accordance with a clear set of ethical standards and guidelines. There are few experiences more powerful in life than seeing your parents standing up for what they believe in, even in the face of ridicule, social ostracism, or personal fear.

Learn Lessons from How You Were Parented

Think about the times you received praise from your parents. What were you doing at the time? Were the praise and acknowledgment the result of educational success? Did you win a race, hit a home run, or score a crucial goal in a soccer game? Was the praise a reward for a clever way you thought up to make money, or perhaps for gaining the upper hand over a competitor in the classroom, playing field, or social arena? Or did your parents give you praise and acknowledgment for positive ethical behavior—for exhibiting compassion and caring for another human being, being generous with your time to a fellow student in need, volunteering to care for a friend's pet, watering your neighbor's garden while they were away on vacation, or simply picking up a piece of trash on the ground?

Use the memories of how *you* were parented to clarify your own parenting goals. First, think about the times you received praise from your own parents, then turn those memories into lessons about what your parents' real values were. Now think about the times *you* give praise and acknowledgment to your own children. Realize that as a parent, nearly everything you do every day of your life is a form of teaching. Every time you smile at your children, every word of encouragement and praise, is a way of teaching them what is truly important to you about who they are and how they behave. The more conscious you are about the lessons you teach them through these moments of praise, the more effectively you can direct the praise to reinforce the ethical behavior and values that you desire.

It is so often the little things of life that make the biggest difference and have the most impact. That is why I will continually urge you to examine your own childhood for parenting lessons about the power of teachable moments. As you look into your own past, you will realize that many of the most important lessons in your life came from unintentional teaching moments with your parents, and probably were experiences that *they* wouldn't even remember at all.

Live As If Today Really Matters

Part of the challenge of raising ethical children is to recognize that every day is another opportunity to reinforce the values we hold dear. Many wise philosophers have taught us to live each day as if it were our last, to imagine each moment as if the fate of the world hung in the balance, and then to ask ourselves how we would act if that were really so. The same is true of parenting. Do your best to act each day with your children as if the example you set *today* will determine the kind of person they will become. Live each day as if the lessons you teach today might be *the* lessons that determine whether or not they will grow up to be ethical human beings. If you could actually live each day with the awareness of the power of your impact on your children, I am convinced that the goal of raising ethical children would be infinitely easier to attain.

The World Children Dream About

Following the devastating impact that the 1992 civil disturbances in Los Angeles had on the emotional lives of children in the L.A. Unified School District, the City of Los Angeles Cultural Affairs Department joined with various schools and their children's choirs to produce a musical video entitled "The World I Dream About." It was an attempt to give children an opportunity to express their hopes and dreams: a world in which violence is no longer an everyday threat; in which thousands of students no longer come to school with guns and knives in their pockets and purses; in which drive-by shootings are a thing of the past (rather than the daily event it is in the lives of many of these children); and in which every boy and girl can grow up in a society that encourages their talents and abilities, nurtures their sense of self-worth and inspires them to fulfill themselves both personally and professionally. I share this with you here, because the need for such a dream is not restricted to riot-torn Los Angeles. It lives in every one of us who cares about children, who cries in our hearts for those left unattended, unloved, uncared for in a hostile world.

Fortunately, most of us can't relate to the cartoon that ran in the *Los Angeles Times* after the 1992 civil disturbances depicting two black children sitting on the steps outside their run-down inner city home. One turns to the other and asks, "What do you want to be if you grow up?"

Fortunately, most of our dreams for our children's future go far beyond whether or not they will survive daily drive-by shootings and gang fights. We have the luxury of assuming they will grow up physically safe and protected. Yet too many continue to focus more on what our children grow up to *do* rather than who they will grow up to *be*. This book is based on the conviction that we should be much more concerned with the kind of person they will become, and much less consumed with the kind of job they will hold. If they are the right kind of person, whatever job or jobs they eventually do will simply be a reflection of who they are. I dream of the day in which children are praised for being kind, considerate, caring, decent human beings, and not only for their academic, athletic, or financial achievements. That, to me, is truly a world worth dreaming about.

Raising ethical children is clearly less a reflection of discovering the right parenting techniques, discipline strategies, or social skills training, and more a function of communicating the right *values*. Who we are and how we live our lives are much more crucial to their ethical development than all the clever parenting strategies and techniques we could ever learn from a book (including this one). That is why I believe that to be successful at raising ethical children you must constantly focus on your goals for your children, that is, on what kind of people you want them to grow up to be.

Set Realistic Goals

It is important for you to have appropriate, realistic goals and expectations for yourself as well as for your children. A "perfect parent" is a contradiction in terms, something you simply never find in the real world. The more you expect yourself to be perfect—the more you think that you must hold yourself to an idealized standard of behavior where you don't make mistakes, never lose your temper, always remain cool and calm, and know exactly the correct response to whatever your children may be doing or saying at the moment—the more you are headed for emotional disaster and parental self-destruction. That is why Dr. Bruno Bettelheim, the world renowned child psychologist and author, entitled his last book on the difficult art of parenting *A Good Enough Parent*. Bettelheim understood that being "good enough" is an achievable goal for everyone, and one that won't drive you crazy in pursuit of an impossible dream.

According to *U.S. News & World Report* (October 27, 1986), a study of 600 adults across the nation by the University of Michigan Institute of Social Research determined that working mothers spent an average of only eleven minutes daily of exclusive play or teaching time (called "quality time") with their children during the weekdays, and about thirty minutes per day on the weekends. Fathers spent about eight minutes of this exclusive quality time with their kids on weekdays, and fourteen minutes on weekends. Even nonworking mothers only spent an average of thirteen minutes per day of exclusive play or teaching time with their kids.

You can imagine what an impossible task parents set out for themselves if they are only willing to commit such a paltry amount of quality time to the upbringing of their children. Time is one of the most precious gifts you can give to another human being, and without it successful parenting takes on all the certainty of a Las Vegas crap table. It is as if you are leaving the success of your child raising up to a roll of the dice, a purely chance experience of hit or miss. If that were your desire, then you wouldn't be reading this book in the first place. So I know that you are the kind of parent who cares deeply about your children and who has a profound commitment to doing your very best to raise them to become caring, loving, ethical human beings.

To that end, I offer a few introductory suggestions that I have found helpful over the years:

1. *Share short rules to live by.* Adults can often be heard to say, "My mother always said . . . " or "My father used to tell me . . . " or "My grandfather's favorite saying was . . . " (In fact, one of my grandfather's favorites was, "Don't wish for fish, fish for fish.") These sayings can be useful ethical guidelines for specific situations, and children appreciate having easy-to-understand aphorisms and sayings.

2. *Point out ethical behavior in others.* Children are surrounded with examples of ethical dilemmas every day—in the newspapers, on television, with friends, family, and strangers on the street. Nearly *every* experience can be an opportunity for ethical decision making. When you realize the world can be a personal "ethics lab," you will be amazed at how many opportunities there are to learn valuable lessons from the people around us.

A recent example of the ethics lab called "life" was found in the powerful television pictures of mothers walking hand in hand with their children to loot local stores during the civil disturbances in Los Angeles in the spring of 1992. This is just one very dramatic example of how daily life is filled with opportunities for morally challenging our children. Of course, part of the frustration of parenting is that ultimately what you and your children learn from any given situation may be very different things, and often the actual learning that does take place is beyond your control.

All you can do is use the situations that are presented to you as best you can. Get your children in the habit of recognizing certain situations as moral dilemmas. If your children are able to point out the moral challenges they see in the newspapers and on television reports, that is half the battle. Certainly, they will be much more ethical decision makers than those who go through life unaware of the dilemmas, conflicts, and important ethical choices and values inherent in everyday activities.

3. *Acknowledge ethical behavior in your children.* Few things are as simple and yet as important as being your children's ethical action cheerleader. Make sure they know that you pay attention to their behavior, and make sure that you cheer when they make positive decisions that reflect good, mature moral judgment. To be an effective cheerleader you must consciously search for opportunities to acknowledge such ethical behavior. It is as simple as "catching them doing something right" (more on this in a later chapter), rather than always focusing on the negatives as is the habit of most parents.

4. *Develop an "ethical action consciousness."* Make yourself into the parent model. As we have already discussed, the *single* most important decision that you can make regarding raising ethical children is to act each day in ways that you would want your children to emulate. Be the best example of ethical behavior you can be. No, you don't have to be perfect, and you shouldn't expect yourself to always have the right answers to every question, or make the right decision in every situation. A good rule of thumb is this: When confronted with an ethical decision, ask yourself how you would want your child to act in the same situation, and you will most often know immediately which choice is the best for you.

Children Ultimately Choose for Themselves

Finally I wish to end this chapter with the wise words of Dr. John White, Associate Professor of Psychiatry at the University of Manitoba. In his book, *Parents in Pain,* he reminds us that our children do not "belong" to us, but rather, are given to us in temporary trust. It is our responsibility to watch over their development, and to give them love, discipline, and moral direction. Yet, regardless of how much we hope and pray that they will in fact lead good, moral, and ethical lives as adults, we also must remember that no matter what we do, ultimately our children remain their own persons, free to choose, free to make their own decisions, free to embrace their own values.

In our next chapter we will turn to the topic of "moral development" and learn from moral development experts how to improve our own ethical parenting skills.

Two

Understanding Moral Development

Education in virtue is the only education which deserves the name.

                                            Plato

Every human being goes through easily recognizable stages of physical development over the course of his or her life. We all understand that the physical attributes and abilities of an infant or a toddler are worlds apart from those of an adolescent or an adult. We all expect our children to pass through these physical stages, slowly learning to master first large and then fine body motor movement. Our children are experiencing the changes in their bodies from childhood to puberty to adulthood, and we hardly give it a second thought.

However, it has only become clear over the past few decades of human research that each of us passes through distinct and identifiable stages of *moral* development as well. No one is born with a fully developed set of innate moral guidelines and standards of ethical behavior. No one comes out of the womb genetically understanding how to make difficult ethical decisions about how to behave in complex social situations. These are *learned* behaviors, reflecting a combination of parental guidance, educational environment, and biological proclivities. Ethical decision making is the result of a complex combination of natural tendencies and social education based on input first from our families, and then from the general social environment in which we live. The most important thing to remember about moral development in children is simply that, according to those experts who study these "stages," morality develops slowly over time.

Human beings are complex, and despite our constant desire for simple, step-by-step directions that will guarantee success in child raising, the innate complexity of human beings, our varied family environments, and social interactions make such automatic predictions impossible. The best we can do is follow general guidelines for

behavior, outline generally agreed-upon steps that will
encourage ethical behavior in children, live the kind of
lives that serve as adequate models of the ethical beings we
desire our children to grow up to become, and then hope
for the best.

What follows, then, is a straightforward presentation of
the basic concepts and generally agreed-upon stages of
moral development in children most widely accepted by
the experts in the field. Although there are some differences of opinion about just how these stages develop and
what exactly constitutes the most important factors that
lead to a child moving smoothly from one stage to the next,
on the whole there seems to be a general agreement that
such stages of moral development do exist in one form or
another.

If you examine the general thrust of how psychologists
describe the process of moral growth and development,
you will discover something of a pattern that seems to hold
almost across the board. It might best be summarized by
the overview of Dr. Lawrence Kohlberg's work captured in
Raising Good Children by Dr. Thomas Lickona. Dr. Lickona
shares his overview of the stages of moral development as
follows:

> The developing person begins by being largely "pre-
> moral": self-centered, following rules only when it's
> in his (sic) interest to do so. In the shift to conven-
> tional morality, the person "joins the group," wants
> to be a "good person" in the conventional, con-
> formist sense of trying to meet the expectations of
> others—either interpersonal others like family or
> friends or impersonal others like one's community,
> institutions, or nation. In the shift to postconven-

tional, principled morality, the individual is no longer completely identified with or locked into the prevailing conventions—the roles, rules, and regulations—of his social system. Now he can mentally stand outside his system, evaluate it, change it if necessary, operating from an independent, principled moral perspective. Is the system just? Does it fully protect human rights? Does it adequately promote the general welfare?

These and other questions form the basis of the decision-making process engaged in by young people searching for answers to difficult and complex moral and ethical questions. At this level the questions themselves reflect a sophistication which tells us that the person asking is already at a very high level of moral reasoning. One of our goals as parents is to do whatever we can to help our children attain this higher stage of moral growth and discernment.

This process of raising ethical children requires the constant reminder that ethical insights come to children in stages, slowly over many years. Parents must realize that they have to talk about ethics and teach their children both by word and action at age-appropriate levels, or they simply will not understand the point you are trying to make. Until they are emotionally, intellectually, and even spiritually ready to experience their greater connection to humanity as a whole, all the preaching in the world is meaningless.

Ethical child raising can be the result of a natural progression of shared experiences, conscious parenting role model moments, and thoughtful talks with your children about how to make the right ethical decisions in different situations that arise in the course of daily living. When you allow the ethical reasoning of your children to progress in a natural but guided fashion from one stage to the next, with your help and your love they will eventually arrive at the appropriate higher stages of ethical development. Now let's examine how children generally move through the stages, and what each stage actually looks like.

Might Makes Right—Stage One

The lowest level of moral development and moral reasoning could be called the "might makes right" level. In this stage "not getting caught," staying out of trouble with adults (who are perceived as all-powerful and generally all-knowing), is the prime motivator for ethical behavior. In a young child of four or five years old, this kind of logic is quite appropriate. In fact, one shouldn't expect much more of young children because they are generally incapable of abstracting any "higher principles" of morality until much later in life.

Some kids still function on this "might makes right" level even after they have become teenagers. Individuals who are functioning at a moral level far below where they rightfully should be suffer from what we might call "arrested moral development." Such a child has simply never grown morally and ethically in a way that keeps pace with his or her physical development. It is just such children who can cause grave problems in school, at home, and in society in general, for they have never internalized an understanding of a moral system that is based on higher principles of common good.

At stage-one reasoning, children simply have no understanding of the practical purpose for rules of behavior within society. They truly don't understand that rules allow society to function smoothly, that rules form the basis of the social contract among society's members, creating a foundation of stability and security within the social structure as a whole. All they know is that rules are made by people in power (usually older and bigger) to keep those weaker (usually younger and smaller) in line, or simply to boss them around. At this stage, the "smart" person seems to be the one who figures out how to get around the rules, how to bend them or twist them so that they can be used to one's advantage while still avoiding getting caught.

What happens at this first stage is that rules are not internalized. They are always seen as an externally imposed condition to be dealt with, manipulated, or gotten around, but never conceptualized as fundamental principles. Morality is perceived as a one-way street—kids are under the control of adults, the younger are under the older, and the weaker are controlled by the stronger. There is no concept of "give and take," of reciprocal relationships in which both parties are able to get some of what they want. Rather, stage one is an "all or nothing" level; the key to moral behavior is power and authority, pure and simple.

You can imagine what it is like when such limited moral vision finds its way into the body of a young adult. In fact, some believe that much of the crime caused by teenagers is the result of such arrested moral development. It is often the root cause of the difficulty that schools, parents, and ultimately the police have in monitoring the behavior and activities of angry, hostile teenagers. They still see "right" and "wrong" primarily as a function of who has the muscle to get what they want.

Tell Your Children "Why"

One way parents can nurture their children's moral development is by giving them at every stage the *reasons* for their desires, *reasons* for their rules, and *reasons* for the consequences that come as a result of breaking those rules. This helps children to make the mental (and emotional) connection between behavior and consequences, and to understand the universality of moral behavior. "Because I said so" is a morally limiting response to a child's question of "Why?" Yet it probably remains the favorite response of most parents (more on this in Chapter 5).

Parenting studies seem to indicate that those parents who primarily focus their demands for ethical behavior on the assertion of their own power as parents, rather than taking the time to help their children work through the moral reasoning involved in their decisions, tend to have children who develop only very low levels of moral understanding. In fact, it is just such parents who unintentionally encourage their children's level of moral reasoning to remain at the "fear of punishment" stage. The trick at every level is to combine appropriate expressions of our own parental authority with explanations of higher-stage moral reasoning.

This sounds a lot more complicated than it is. In fact, it is simply what good parents have been doing for generations—taking the time, patience, care, and love to point out to their children *why* it's important to treat others with kindness and compassion, *why* it's important not to steal things from other people, *why* it's important to tell the truth and be the kind of person whom others trust. Good parents have always done just that, and the acknowledgment of this by the moral development "experts" in the field simply attests to the fact that one doesn't need a Ph.D. in Ethical Parenting to raise ethical children. What one does need is to be a loving, caring, nurturing, aware parent who is willing to take the time necessary to teach your children both by word of mouth and living example the relationship between ethical behavior, on the one hand, and creating the kind of world in which we all would like to live, on the other. One of the things that I want to reinforce as strongly as possible is that it is never too soon to teach your children the enduring value of social responsibility, and you can never reinforce it too often.

With every stage of moral development that is attained, children add yet another piece to the ultimate puzzle of understanding the ethical principles that forge a society of potentially competing individuals into a cohesive and interlocking whole. As children go through these various stages of moral reasoning and development, each stage reveals a partial understanding of the broader picture of morality and ethics leading to the discoveries of the next.

An Eye for an Eye—Stage Two

After children have passed through the lowest stages of moral reasoning, they arrive at the level with which Biblical readers will be familiar: "an eye for an eye, and a tooth for a tooth." If someone punches you in the arm, at this level of understanding you feel compelled to punch him back. If someone steals your notebook, you steal hers in return. It is the principle of equal and exact revenge, and with children you will notice that *everything* has to get paid back or else life isn't fair. It is somehow out of balance, whether you are dealing with a physical injury, a verbal abuse, or simply someone making a mean face.

By the same token, just as this is the stage of exacting revenge in kind for damages (real or imagined), it is also the time in which those who do something good to you have to be paid back as well. The moral ledger sheet must always be in balance when a child is at this stage of moral development, whether on the positive or negative side, for it is the equal, fair treatment that is the key.

Children Want Everything to Be Fair

You have probably noticed that very young children seem to live lives full of moral indignation. When they function on this second level of moral reasoning, they believe that things ought to be "fair." To a child, being fair usually translates as being equal. Equal punishments are expected for equal infractions of rules. They believe that if they get punished for breaking a certain rule, then so should everyone else. When this doesn't happen, children react with their own version of moral outrage. They may yell and scream, throw a tantrum, or cry. No matter what form the reaction takes, the fundamental principles are usually the same. What often happens is that on some level children internalize the apparent disparity in consequences of behavior and subsequently feel that they are worth less as human beings than other kids.

Of course, at this stage children often think that what fair really means is getting what they want. At this stage of intellectual and moral awareness, kids think that the whole world exists simply to serve them. At the next stage, children begin to realize that there are also rules that have to be followed whether or not you like them. Then they begin to recognize that fairness involves more than simply following the rules that adults have arbitrarily decided upon, but that the rules, too, are based on broader principles of fairness, equality, and justice.

Another important concept to teach kids regarding fairness is to tell them that treatment that is fair does not necessarily mean "equal" or "the same"—it may rather mean giving someone what they *need*. One child may need a sweater and another a book, but since everyone doesn't necessarily need exactly the same things all the time, it isn't necessary for everyone to get the same things.

This level of moral development also represents a very concrete stage of understanding. Children only understand things as being right or wrong according to their ability to *see* the results of their behavior. They are generally not yet capable of the kind of abstract thinking required to understand the universal implications of ethics and morality for society. You can't expect a child at this stage either to realize that if he or she lies, or cheats or steals from someone, it undermines the foundation of integrity and trust, and the expectation of honesty and forthright behavior that is a necessary component of a just society.

Building Moral Reasoning

Such concepts as "trust" and "integrity" are simply beyond the intellectual level of young children to understand. They still function in the very real, concrete, and physical "If I can touch it or see it I know it is there" world of limited ethical understanding. Your job as the parent is to teach your children higher levels of moral thinking, by demonstrating examples of proper ethical behavior coupled with a higher-level explanation as to *why* you act the way you do.

For example, when a neighbor accidently leaves a pair of sunglasses at your house, take your child with you as you return the lost item to its rightful owner. On the way over, you may point out to your inquisitive child that it is important for you to return the sunglasses to Mr. Clay down the street, because you wouldn't want to live in a city in which people kept other people's things. You might even ask your child to imagine what the world would be like if you couldn't ever trust your neighbors to be honest and return lost things that belong to you when they found them. This helps to stretch the child's understanding of the reasons for practicing ethical actions from one stage of moral development on to the next.

This is an important step in the overall process of moral education and raising ethical children because parents need to constantly provide not only moral guidance, but *moral reasoning* as well. Children respond better, more fully and wholeheartedly, when they are treated with dignity and respect, regardless of their age.

Another important reason for taking the time to provide explanations, reasons, and moral justifications for the ethical choices that you make is that it is an important way in which parents can demonstrate respect for their children.

Among other benefits to your children, the very process of giving such explanations enhances their self-esteem. This is because they inevitably feel important and worthwhile whenever you bestow your two most valuable and precious possessions on them—your *time* and your *attention*. This is also an important method for teaching your children respect for others. When we are treated with respect and dignity by others, it much more easily becomes a natural habit to repay that dignity and respect in return.

An added benefit of consistently demonstrating that who your children are and what they have to say is important to you is that when they are treated with respect, they are much less likely to spend a lot of energy sneaking around behind your back to avoid getting caught. Obviously your goal is to raise open, honest, unintimidated children who know that they will get a fair shake with you, that you will listen honestly to their point of view, and that you are willing to compromise and admit when they are right. Such kids are much more likely to share their problems honestly with you, and to tell you what they are thinking about doing rather than simply doing it first and then spending a lot of their time figuring out how to keep you from finding out. In this way you encourage the development of the moral quality of honesty, and avoid training your children to see their parents, and all sources and symbols of authority as powers to be avoided and manipulated for their own ends.

As children grow morally from one stage to another, they gradually leave the tightly controlled world of self-centeredness and self-gratification, and expand their emotional horizons to include the feelings of others. This path of moral growth and development entails a constantly growing and expanding realization of the interconnectedness of all human beings and the many complex relationships that bind us all together. Moving from this stage of moral development into the next is actually a giant leap forward into the gaping chasm of moral responsibility. It is a time in which the light dawns to reveal that a new form of thinking is necessary which includes a growing concern for the welfare of others.

In the end, the success of your ability to help move your children along the moral development path from one stage to the next is primarily dependent upon developing a relationship with them that is based on love, trust, integrity, understanding, openness, and forgiveness. These are crucial tools in the ongoing battle for the moral minds and hearts of our children. All of us want to have the kind of relationships with our children that are so filled with love and acceptance that when we disagree with or discipline them, or when we point out where they acted inappropriately or were wrong, they know that what we are saying is based on our unconditional regard for their emotional health and well-being.

Relationships Take Time

Few of us would suggest that parents can suddenly appear full-blown in their children's lives when they are reaching for adulthood and expect that such moral and ethical guidance, caring, support, and love would be accepted without question. Relationships take time to build and develop. They obviously have the best chance for success when enough time is spent interacting in a thousand little ways that together can weave the fabric of a loving, nurturing, teaching relationship. Your joint activities may be as simple as taking a walk on the beach, having a picnic, going to a sporting event, visiting the local library and reading together, or seeing a movie or a play.

The important thing is to create whatever opportunities you can to have one-on-one focused family time with each of your children. Then you will have laid the groundwork so that when you do give advice, you have enough credibility with your child and he or she is able to accept criticisms and suggestions and use them for self-improvement.

Even while in the midst of establishing that credibility with your children through an ongoing consistency of word and deed, you must do whatever you can to constantly help them to move forward along the path of moral and ethical development. Your goal is to encourage your children to experience a sense of connection with other human beings of all ages (and ideally all religions, races, nationalities, and genders as well). You want them to empathize with others at the basic gut level—to feel their sorrows and joys, their frustrations and triumphs.

Appealing to a Higher Moral Level

In order to stretch your children's ability to empathize with the needs, feelings, and concerns of others, you must consciously appeal to higher levels of moral reasoning than the simple level of fairness, equal treatment, or reciprocity. When you ask your children to do something for you or another member of the family, you might appeal to *love*— a higher stage of ethical or moral reasoning—rather than mere reciprocity ("Do this for me because I did that for you")—a much lower stage. You might direct your children to behave in certain ways because that is what you expect from anyone who is a competent human being, or because such behavior is simply what is expected of anyone who is a member of your family.

Another important key to encouraging moral growth and development is to appeal to religious values that are based on doing for others because it's "the right thing to do," not just because you expect them to do it for you. "Love your neighbor as yourself" is probably the simplest yet most profound statement of ethical empathic behavior that the Judeo-Christian tradition teaches, and you can reinforce that powerful and important lesson over and over again. (For a full discussion of this, see Chapter 4.)

Raising ethical children is inevitably a balancing act. It is a complex, challenging experiment in parenting with no guarantee of success in the long run. It requires striking a delicate balance between holding on and letting go, exercising control and granting freedom, giving guidance as well as independence, and protecting your children from negative peer pressure while allowing them opportunities to explore the world on their own terms.

The Moral Mirror of Others—Stage Three

One of the realities that you can help adolescents to come to grips with is that their sense of personal value is, to a degree much larger than they might admit, dependent upon the moral and ethical judgments of others. To some degree, each of us relies upon the reflection of our own behavior that we see mirrored in the faces, words, and actions of those around us for our judgment of what is right and what is wrong about our own behavior. This fact carries within it both positives and negatives, which you can understand and teach to your children.

On the positive side, your children will learn that one reason to be a good person is so that they will think well of themselves and have others think highly of them as well. On the negative side, there is a tendency to turn one's own ethical judgments over entirely to peers, parents, and teachers, thereby abdicating personal responsibility for our actions and their consequences. Since children inevitably want the approval of their peers and parents, at this stage one of the moral challenges that they face is how to incorporate enough of the general moral expectations of society into their own ethical values system, without allowing these outside social forces to dictate their own inner conscience as well.

Hopefully, as your children grow through their adolescent years, the foundation of ethical decision making that you have established through your own parent talk and daily example will help create a strong basis upon which your children will eventually establish their own secure moral self-image. This "ethical identity" will ultimately only be successful if it can stand on its own, regardless of the social/moral/ethical expectations and mores of your children's peers. Of course, the bad news is that ultimately only time will truly tell whether you have been successful in providing them with a solid foundation from which to build a strong ethical identity.

Internalized Ethical Self-Image—Stage Four

In the normal course of human growth and development, as your children grow and mature morally, their understanding that ethical behavior grows purely out of a "tit-for-tat" model of human interaction ("I will be good so that others will be good to me") is transformed into this internalized ethical self-image. At this level, being a good person, acting in a moral fashion becomes simply an expression of living up to an internalized standard of behavior that has come to represent the highest and best aspects of your children's personality and self-concept.

When children reach this stage of moral development, they develop the capacity for moral empathy, for putting themselves in another's shoes and experiencing how that person might feel in any given situation. This allows them to introduce an element of moral flexibility into their decision-making process. Now the world is seen less and less in terms of absolutes, black and white, good guys and bad guys, and more and more as a stage upon which players struggle with their consciences, attempting to do the right thing even though they may often make mistakes and wrong choices. Justice begins to be tempered with mercy and compassion, and your children begin to appreciate the moral ambiguity inherent in so many of life's daily struggles, choices, and ethical situations.

The next step along the moral development path takes young people from an ethical reasoning that focuses on questions like "What does it mean to be a good son or daughter, friend, and so on?" to a more complex level of reasoning where they begin to develop the recognition that they are part of a larger social system. At this stage the questions increasingly evolve into "What does it mean to be a good member of my group/community/town/religion/society?"

Social Obligation—Stage Five

With their exploration of what it means to be part of a larger social system, young people begin to figure out that they are part of an integrated social network. Being part of that interlocking social fabric means doing their part to hold up their end of the social contract so that society can continue to function smoothly. Their personal responsibility projects large on the screen of society, and they experience probably for the first time the weight of social obligation that comes with being a participating member of a social group.

It is only at this fifth stage of ethical reasoning that children are able to truly understand what good citizenship in a society demands of them. Only then can they appreciate all the intricate social rules that people agree upon (consciously or not), that allow society as a whole to continue to function under any circumstances. "Social obligation" becomes a more demanding master than even peer pressure. Young people begin to realize that it isn't good for people to just go along with whatever society has to offer; they must actively contribute something back to their society or community or we will eventually revert to the jungle of amoral social violence and apathy.

Human beings at all ages are complex, multifaceted, and fascinating. It is impossible, no matter how much study and research goes into the data, to predict with 100 percent accuracy how anyone will act at any given time in any specific circumstance. When we move to higher levels of moral reasoning, we don't simply shed our previous understandings and moral levels at the door like some ethical reptile. Instead, we somehow take the new knowledge, new understanding of life, new interpretations of what things *mean* in the world, and integrate them into our newly emerging realities.

An Ethical Reality Test

Kids begin to ask how their actions will affect others in the social system. They begin to feel responsible for more than their own tiny sphere of influence. They contemplate what life would be like if everyone acted in a certain way. They ask themselves "What would the world be like if everyone acted just the way I do?" and hope that the answer they receive is a positive and encouraging one. Using this "ethical reality projection" test as a criterion for ethical behavior is actually not such a bad idea to share with your children. I have often found that it is one of the most easily understood, concrete ways of measuring ethical decisions, and one which teenagers find particularly compelling.

When young people reach their teen years they are often torn between the competing interests of powerful peer pressures, and the desire to be "independent" thinkers and stand on their own. They are, on the one hand, easily influenced by the likes and dislikes, fads, and popular culture of their friends, while on the other hand they are searching for self-identity which encourages them to find some way to stand out from the crowd.

It is precisely because of this constant emotional moral tug-of-war that teenagers are particularly responsive to the compelling logic of holding themselves to the "What would the world be like if everyone did what I am thinking of doing" standard of behavior. They can often (but not always) see that being truly socially responsible means acting in such a way that *they* can serve as models of correct and appropriate ethical behavior for others, even as they must look to those who are older and more experienced than themselves for their own ethical models.

Embracing Religion

The same holds true in the realm of religion. Here, too, children express various stages of moral clarity and vision that correspond to the level of their spiritual and ethical growth and development.

At earlier stages of moral development, religion is perceived in such a way that children may go to church at first merely to please parents or God, and then because it makes them feel like better people. Higher stages of moral development find the same people now thinking about the effects of their actions on the larger community, and feeling drawn in kinship to a community of believers who share their moral code. Ultimately, people are able to discover a common faith community through which they are able to work out their own relationship with God, the performance of godly deeds, and the full expression of their beliefs.

At this higher stage of development, people also understand for the first time the true importance of self-respect. They make decisions based on wanting to feel good about themselves, being a person whose word can be trusted, demonstrating integrity in their behavior and actions toward others, and being the kind of person who others know keeps his or her promises and can be counted upon. All of these attributes are seen as not only desirable but necessary, first, in order for others to hold them in high esteem, and second, to bring themselves closer to their own moral ideal.

Encouraging Independence

One of the simplest ways that you can help your children to move to this higher stage of moral reasoning is to encourage them in every way to develop a sense of independence and an ability to make decisions on their own. Second, you can take the time to constantly help your children to be aware of and understand their place in the larger social context. Teach your children about the different levels of society into which all of us fit. Participating in Boy Scouts or Girl Scouts, soccer or little league, church or synagogue, youth groups, cheerleading or playing on a school team, community-wide opportunities, or countless other activities allows us the flexibility to live our lives in concentric circles, with many diverse interests interlocking at the same time.

Simple Rules for Complex Choices

Finally, you can introduce your children into the world of complex social systems beyond their own family and friends. Point out to them the various alternatives that are possible when involved in decision making. Give examples of positive self-regard, demonstrations of self-respect, and simple rules to live by that they can latch onto for support and inspiration. For example, the simple rule I have always given my daughter, Gable, when she is faced with a behavioral decision that involves another person is, "Would it be OK with you if the situation were reversed, and the other person acted toward you the way you are planning to act toward him or her?" If the answer is "yes," then it's a pretty safe bet that whatever behavior she is contemplating will be fine.

Another approach is a form of simple imaginary role playing. Ask your kids to imagine they were the other person in any two-way argument or discussion, and see how they think the other person's point of view might be expressed and explained. Have them argue the opposite view from the one they are espousing, "as if" they were passionately committed to it, and they will be surprised at how easily they can develop a sense of empathy and understanding for another's point of view.

A third technique is to ask them to play, "How would you feel if . . . ?" For example, "If you were a substitute teacher, how would you feel if the class acted in a disruptive and rude manner?" Or perhaps, "If you owned the local camera store, how would you feel if someone came in and stole a camera or some film?" This helps get them out of their usual modes of thinking and forces them to see the world from another person's perspective and imagined life experience. In this way you are broadening their ability to approach any given problem from a variety of angles, teaching them the importance of viewing an issue from as many sides as possible, and expanding their understanding of the diversity of opinion that exists in people whose life experiences are different from their own.

Another way of encouraging children to see themselves in the context of a larger social system is to spend time sharing with them stories about the world outside their town, or state, or country. Expose them to movies, television shows, books, and magazines that will give them an appreciation for life in the world beyond their own limited sphere of understanding and experience. Talk about current events and important or challenging situations that are happening in the world, and involve your children in making ethical choices and moral decisions and taking positions on the important social and political issues of the day.

It isn't important for you to be able to give your children the "right" answers to complex moral questions. What is important is that you engage them in the process of examining issues and realizing that they are in fact complex in the first place. What happens all too often is that all of us fall into the trap of wanting to simplify life beyond its capacity to be simplified. We seem to prefer straightforward problems with "yes" or "no" answers, when the truth is usually some gray area in between. The key is to help them learn to live with the real ambiguities of life, to celebrate the complexity of it all, and to even feel OK about the apparent paradoxes within our own thinking.

Most important always is how you *act* when it comes to these complex social issues. Do your children see you giving time to community service; being involved with issues of hunger, the homeless, and the environment; voting in elections; contributing to charities; and demonstrating a social and political awareness and sense of responsibility to supporting society? If they don't, how can you expect that they will suddenly develop a social conscience of their own? Why should they take part in improving society and the world in which we live, unless they have seen you leading the way? Never forget that *you* are their primary, most important, and most influential role model, *always*.

Spiritual Democracy and Personal Responsibility—Stage Six

One of your greatest and most important challenges is to teach your children that one of the highest forms of moral reasoning occurs when an individual can look past the self, and understand that society is based on universal principles that unite all people simply because they are human beings. This stage of moral development holds as its foundation for ethical behavior, the principle of respect for the inalienable rights of individuals. These are rights that are ours simply by reason of birth, regardless of social standing, intelligence, country of origin, race, or religion. They must really be contained within the very definition of what it means to be a human being.

This is what I like to think of as the ultimate level of spiritual democracy. For the inevitable result of this line of thinking is the realization that all persons, regardless of their status in life, deserve to be treated as moral equals. This level of moral thinking allows the individual to step outside any given political or social system to evaluate that system on the basis of how well it is respecting, encouraging or nurturing individual human rights, justice, and personal responsibility.

It is only when an individual functions at this ethical level that the concept of "civil disobedience" can have any meaning, for it implies that one is held to a higher moral standard than simply social good, or that which encourages the smooth functioning of society.

The Martin Luther King, Jrs and Mohandas Gandhis of the world functioned at this level of moral and ethical integrity, but so do countless unnamed compassionate, caring, ethical human beings whom we encounter every day of our lives. Our goal is to help raise the level of moral discourse within our families, our churches and synagogues, our schools, political forums, books, magazines and television shows so that our children naturally aspire to create a world that supports, sustains, and empowers the individual to self-actualization and fulfillment.

This is the level of true democracy, of respect for diversity and cultural pluralism. It is to this moral level that our political system allegedly aspires, and that our social system claims to champion—the individual pursuit of life, liberty, and happiness. It is an appeal to a higher moral order, and it is indeed the goal of ethical parenting. Moreover, we actually want our children to see this vision of a moral, democratic, equitable world as the goal of the society that they can help to create.

We want our children to create a shared vision of a world that encourages each and every human being to fulfill his or her own unique potential. That is truly the highest good, and it is actually within our power as parents to pass on to our children. Human beings desperately want to share a common vision. They virtually cry out for inspiration—to be shown a picture through words and deeds of a society worth supporting; worth committing our selves to; worth building with our own blood, sweat, and tears.

This then, is an overview of the stages of moral development and growth. Each of us as parents shares the desire for our own children to reach for the stars, to fulfill themselves as individuals and as members of society within the context of loving, caring, nurturing and empowering relationships. It is our responsibility to help set them on the right path and do our best to guide them down the road to personal fulfillment and self-actualization. Ultimately, all we can do is the best that we can do, and the rest, of course, is up to them.

Three

Discipline Guidelines and Moral Decision Making

A punishment is something that a parent does to you. A consequence is something you do to yourself.

Carin, 8 years old

One of the great challenges of ethical parenthood is learning to love our children even when they are acting unlovable. When children's actions are rebellious, rude, or obnoxious, they can quite often be attributed to the important childhood job of testing our limits of tolerance and their limits of acceptable behavior. Dr. Bruno Bettelheim, the world famous psychologist who taught at the University of Chicago, once said that any time a parent permits a child to talk back or put the parent down, it belittles or degrades the parent. But the more serious damage is actually being done to the child. This is because our children's own inner sense of security is, in part, the result of having parents they can trust and look to for strength and guidance. When parents allow themselves to be belittled or degraded by their children, it undermines that very sense of security that is so crucial to the well-being of our children.

Raising ethical children requires that we create the kind of environment in our homes that is conducive to ethical behavior. Ethical behavior from children toward parents is necessary, but equally important is the flow from parents to children. As I have already stated, you are your children's primary role model in life, whether or not you want it that way. Therefore, you are ethically responsible for setting the moral tone and climate in your home, for defining what is and is not acceptable behavior from your children, and the kind of behavior that you will and will not tolerate in their relationships with each other, with other members of the family, and with you.

You are also responsible for setting the limits of the nature of the relationships that exist within your family system. Obviously parents want to be on good, trusting, open terms with their children. However, at the same time they don't want to be their "friend," at least not until they have grown into adults themselves. This is important because parents need to be the source of discipline, guidance, security, and moral strength for their children, which is not the role played by friends. Put another way, if you become a "pal" to your children most of the time, when the need arises for you to discipline, teach, or insist on specific behavior from them, why should they listen to a "pal's" demands? If you pretend that you have an equal relationship, it undermines the essential nature of the parent–child guidance and discipline relationship.

All this doesn't mean that you have to be cold, aloof, or distant from your children. Quite the contrary is true. Children will respond best to parents who have already demonstrated they are reasonable and willing to listen, rather than purely autocratic and unbending. Children will inevitably find it easier to listen to parents who have shown a capacity to empathize with the struggles, emotional traumas, and difficult decisions that childhood demands.

The Essence of Discipline

Discipline, simply put, is teaching a child the way he or she should act. According to Dr. Howard Hendricks in *Family Happiness Is Homemade,* the secret to having a disciplined child is to be a disciplined parent. Unfortunately in our modern age, too often parents misunderstand the idea of discipline and think it means punishment. Nothing could be farther from the truth. Discipline involves everything you do to help your children learn to be the kind of person you want them to become. It is training, positive reinforcement of desired behavior, rewards to encourage positive self-esteem, and demonstrations of correct social and ethical behavioral expectations. In short, discipline involves everything that a parent does that is designed to produce a whole, fulfilled, ethical person who is ready and able to engage in a process of life-long growth and learning toward the ultimate goal of maturation, self-actualization, and fulfillment.

Naturally, there are many roads that lead to this ultimate goal. If you read everything ever written about discipline and child raising, you would probably find half a dozen responsible and respected "experts" in the field who give various differing recommendations and guidelines for behavior. Raising children is not an exact science. It is more like an art form, where there are general rules and guidelines that everyone who pays any attention at all knows are important, and then there are a hundred different ways that individuals interpret and express those guidelines and rules.

You Teach by Example

When you strip away all of the veneer that surrounds these various discipline and decision-making models, you are ultimately confronted with a crucial and universal reality: *everything you do* teaches by example. You are constantly demonstrating to your children your values, your goals, and your ethical standards by your own daily behavior—whether or not you want to.

Whether you take a positive nurturing approach to discipline, or an erratic, explosive, and emotionally damaging approach, you will be teaching a whole series of lessons about self-esteem, parent–child relationships, how to parent, and acceptable ethical behavior that your child will internalize. The idea of this book is simply to help you engage in that automatic daily activity of role modeling for your child the kind of behavior you ultimately desire, in as self-aware and conscious a manner as possible. I want you to make the kind of parenting choices for your child each day that you will be able to look back on each night with satisfaction and approval.

The worst thing is for parents to tell me, "I know I shouldn't act that way with my child, but I just keep losing it. I lost sight of the impact I am having. I hold things in and bottle up my feelings until they simply erupt out of my control, making an emotional mess all over the place. I wish I had some clear steps for coping with the ups and downs of parenting that would at least give me some guideposts that I can refer to when I begin to get stressed out on parenting."

That is exactly what this book is for. It is designed to serve as a constant reference for those difficult moments. Take a deep breath, lock yourself in the bathroom if you must, open this book and look at the sections that outline specific steps to take in addressing difficult moments with your child.

Creating a "Success Journal"

Naturally, your goal is to live your life on a daily basis so that you are automatically the kind of model you desire for your children to follow. Unfortunately, the reality of parenting is that nothing happens quite so smoothly and cleanly as all that. Every family, every child, every parent has ups and downs, good days and bad days, moments of emotional overload and days when everything just seems to be going beautifully and you can't imagine that it will ever be difficult again.

One of the techniques that I have found very helpful to parents in getting through those moments of frustration and upset is to keep a "Success Journal." This can be a ringed binder, notebook, pad of paper, manila folder, or whatever is convenient for you, in which you write down the stories of your successful parenting moments. Write about any time, no matter how short or long, in which you felt good about your own parenting choices, or had a positive parent-child interaction, or felt like you taught something positive to your children. You might write about a morning in which everything went smoothly, or a bedtime experience that was warm, positive, and loving for you and your child.

Once you have made entries in your Success Journal for a while, whenever things get rough, you can take it out and read about your own successes of the past. It will remind you that you do in fact have positive parenting skills, and that you have been in the past and will be in the future successful as a parent.

Review your journal, then take a few moments to recollect your thoughts and remind yourself of the kind of parent you want to be. Recall the image you want to project to your children, and then emotionally regroup and begin to take the necessary steps to become the kind of parent you want your children to grow up to emulate. No, it isn't easy to remain calm in the midst of feeling angry because your children are misbehaving. Maybe you are feeling frustrated because it seems that they actually go out of their way to defy you (which, of course, is sometimes absolutely true), but after all is said and done, *you* are the adult and *they* are the children.

You Are the Parent

All too often it seems, parents act as if they actually aren't sure who is the parent. They give up their sense of authority, treat their children like peers, and suffer the consequences. Hopefully this chapter will dissuade you from pursuing the ill-conceived idea that your job is to befriend your children—it isn't. It is to give them guidance, support, caring, clear direction, and unconditional love. Once you have accomplished that, then perhaps at some time in the future when they have grown into adults, you can create a loving and mutually supportive way to become your children's friend as well.

The Outside Expert

Another technique that I have often suggested to parents is the "Outside Expert," and it involves just a bit of creative imagination. I tell parents to imagine that they have an invisible parenting expert who is magically on call 24 hours a day, 7 days a week, 52 weeks a year. This expert (you can give her or him a name if it makes it more concrete and easier to visualize) will magically appear by your side at any time that you call to give you advice, remind you of the parenting skills that you already know but are perhaps overlooking in the midst of your current emotional upset, or simply point out the negative consequences of the parenting behavior that you are currently exhibiting.

I tell people to use this outside expert whenever they are in need of short circuiting an emotional parenting crisis. Some people find it easier to do this process by actually imagining a real parenting expert like Dr. Benjamin Spock, Dr. Joyce Brothers, or Dear Abby (or even Dr. Reuben). It is really a very simple and easy thing to do. You use this magical expert to help you to step out of your own narrowly focused emotional state, and view the interaction between you and your child from a more objective, impersonal point of view.

Whenever you feel yourself beginning to get out of control or to lose your perspective, call on your expert. As you take three slow deep breaths, imagine what he or she would say to you about what you are doing. Imagine the advice you would be getting if your expert were actually in the room watching what was happening between you and your child.

Most of the time, you already know what would be the best and most appropriate way of dealing with the specific situation you are facing. It is usually just that you have allowed your emotional upset to interfere with your own best judgment. That is why this magical outside expert works so well. When you call on the "Doctor" of your choice, you are allowing your own best sense and inner guide to re-emerge from behind the emotional wall that you have temporarily erected out of your anger or frustration. Then you can listen to your own best instincts, and follow the advice that you know you would give yourself anyway.

In fact, this is one of the best methods for reminding yourself of the parenting skills and child-raising techniques that you already know. When you are upset, confused, feeling overwhelmed, or in any way out of control, simply imagine that someone in your exact situation has come to *you* for advice on how to interact with *their* children. Imagine what you would tell them. My experience is that 99.9 percent of the time you will be giving exactly the correct answer for yourself as well.

In this way you can create an island of objectivity in the midst of the stormy seas of what might otherwise be a potentially destructive emotional situation. Creating ways to tune in to your own inner self, to allow your own best judgments to express themselves and overshadow the emotional overload that you are feeling, is a crucial skill that can empower you with the tools to be in control of your parenting experiences with your child.

Children Want Discipline

These are absolutely essential skills to learn if you are going to raise a caring, compassionate, emotionally secure, and ethically committed child. Over a decade ago, a 1980 Gallup poll of graduating high school seniors revealed that they wished their parents and teachers had loved them enough to discipline them more and require more of them. These students knew that this was their parents' role and responsibility, and that whether or not it was "fun," whether or not they liked it, such clear guidelines and expectations were exactly what they needed to grow into emotionally mature and highly functioning adults.

The wonderful truth is, that when you teach children discipline, you give them one of the most important tools for future success and happiness that is possible to give. With proper loving discipline, you empower your child to function on a high level in society and to have a strong inner sense of self and well-being that is absolutely essential for any future success as an adult or as a parent.

The disciplined person is the one who does what needs to be done, when it needs to be done, regardless of whether it is fun, or easy, or convenient to do so. In fact, anyone who has ever accomplished anything in life has done so through the ability to exhibit an inner discipline. Anyone who creates anything of beauty, whether it be a painting, a piece of music, a book, an article—or a child— has had to have the discipline necessary to set the appropriate goals and the follow-through to make those goals a reality.

That is why creating an atmosphere of consistent, reliable discipline is so important to the emotional health, well-being, and success of your children. By creating clear guidelines and expectations of ethical and moral behavior, by demonstrating in your daily life that you, too, believe that such guidelines for behavior are important, you are providing your children with the keys to competence that are so important for their future success.

Children Need to Experience Competence

Every child needs experiences of competence both large and small that demonstrate that they can accomplish tasks entrusted to them, and can be counted on to finish a challenge successfully. It doesn't really matter what the responsibility is, how complex it may be, or how long it takes to accomplish the goal. What is important is that the task be something that is possible for the child to accomplish. This is crucial so that the overall experience is one of self-satisfaction and an inner sense of success and accomplishment.

One of the first steps to raising positive, ethical children is to teach them from an early age the importance of doing even little things around the house. In this way, one step at a time, they naturally progress into accepting more and more responsibility. Success builds upon success, one experience of competence builds upon the previous experience, until you have literally instilled within your children the unassailable certainty that they can accomplish just about anything that they choose to tackle in life. That is truly a great mark of success, and will open up wonderful worlds of willing experimentation for your children, along with an openness to taking on new challenges without becoming paralyzed by the fear of failure.

Making Values Clear

Studies on the self-esteem of children seem to indicate that children with high self-esteem generally have parents who run a tight ship with a clearly defined and comprehensive set of rules, which are usually consistently enforced. Such findings suggest that parents who have definite values, who have a clear idea of what they regard as appropriate behavior, and who make these beliefs known to their children are more likely to rear children who value themselves highly, develop their own sense of ethics, and have greater respect and affection for their parents.

When parents don't assume this responsibility, their children are apt to interpret this as a symbol of parental indifference. According to the results of the Coopersmith study, such lack of clearly expressed values and guidelines has a tendency to create anxiety in children, while at the same time reducing their capacity to develop strong inner controls over their own behavior.

Catch Them Doing Something Right

Parents who raise successful ethical children have developed in their children over many years the expectation that their behavior is important to their parents. Children must expect that when they do something wrong—when they act out inappropriately, when they misbehave whether in private or public—their parents will correct them and respond with a previously understood set of guidelines and rules for discipline.

At the same time, it is equally if not more important for parents to recognize and acknowledge *positive* behavior in their children. One of the greatest tragedies of child raising is that most parents only react to their children when they do something bad. Since for kids, parental attention is one of the most basic and important forms of reward and acknowledgment, it stands to reason that such parental behavior only encourages improper behavior, and discourages appropriate behavior.

That is exactly why I believe that one of the best and most important positive parenting techniques is to make a pledge to catch your children doing something right each day. Through this constant reinforcement of their positive, desirable behavior parents can have one of the most lasting and profound effects on establishing both self-esteem and patterns of proper behavior in their children. This daily dose of positive attention, will in effect encourage your children to expect that you will notice and pay attention to them when they are behaving properly, just as you pay attention and give acknowledgment (albeit negative) when they behave improperly.

Most parents simply ignore good behavior altogether, assuming that their children are fully conversant with all parental expectations of how they should act in any given situation. The truth is, your children need encouragement to remember what your expectations are. More than that, they need to experience firsthand that they will receive a bigger reward—more of your attention (and that attention will feel a whole lot better)—by simply behaving properly than they will by misbehaving.

This is truly one of the single most essential, most crucial steps in the entire parenting process. Unfortunately, as important as it is, most parents seem uncomfortable with the idea. Either they dismiss it immediately out of hand, or they gloss over the idea lightly and then reject it. It is almost as if parents are afraid to let their children know that they appreciate good behavior. Some parents think that they might spoil their children by giving them too much praise or acknowledgment.

In my opinion, you can't overacknowledge your children. They need your approval as much as the air they breathe or the food they eat. They need you to let them know not only when they are doing something wrong, but when they do something right as well. Imagine what kind of world it would be if every parent went on a "Do Right Treasure Hunt," where every day they set out to find as many things that their children do right as they can, and then to make sure their kids hear about it.

The Legend of One Hundred Blessings

There is an ancient Jewish legend that says the world will be complete when everyone discovers one hundred blessings in their lives each day. I love to tell parents this legend, and then challenge them to do the same with their own children—find one hundred opportunities each day to tell their kids about something they did that made their parents proud of them. Give it a try for a week or two, and see how it transforms your relationships with your children and the entire mood around the house. And, of course, watch out that you don't slip back into the all-too-typical deadly parenting mode of simply ignoring your children until they misbehave. If you think about the messages that you want to convey to your children regarding what constitutes desired behavior, you can't go wrong.

The Lure of Negative Attention

I'm sure you have had similar experiences as a student (or even a teacher if you've ever been one), when it comes to how teachers relate to children in the classroom. It very quickly becomes an expected and natural (even if negative) aspect of your child's school experience to expect that the only behavior that will elicit a reaction from a teacher is negative behavior.

Teachers, like parents, find it easiest to ignore children as long as they are not calling attention to themselves by misbehaving. As long as they remain quiet and work and play well with others, they are usually all but ignored and overlooked by their teachers. When I was a child in elementary school, I was the kind of kid whose name every teacher knew by the end of the first day of class. I guarantee it wasn't because of my model behavior, either!

When a child is very active, has trouble sitting still, or has the bad habit of calling out answers and jumping in to participate even when not called upon (all of which I was consistently guilty), teachers can't help but notice them and react to their interruptions. Very soon a pattern of expectations develops in which the teacher comes to expect a certain level of participation (whether or not called for) from the student, watches him or her closer than others, and reacts more quickly than might otherwise occur to perceived misbehavior, and the cycle continues.

Students quickly learn that it is the ones who stand out by acting out in class, by talking out of turn, by never sitting still, or by playing with their neighbor when they are supposed to be listening, who get all the attention. These are the students whose names are inevitably the first learned by the teachers. The good, quiet, well-behaved students are usually close to invisible.

Since we recognize that it is a fundamental human characteristic to want and need attention and acknowledgment, it's obvious that responding primarily to negative behavior is a fundamentally flawed and extremely negative approach to both teaching and parenting. Such teaching and parenting styles (typical though they might be) constantly encourage children to act out and misbehave.

As it is with teachers in the classroom, so it is with parents at home. The more you ignore positive behavior, the more your children will search for acknowledgment and recognition in negative ways. If you only notice them when they are bad, they quickly learn that it pays to be bad. After all, even though it may be a bit uncomfortable to be yelled at and reprimanded by one's parents, it is infinitely more desirable than being ignored altogether. That is one of the most important parenting lessons that any of us can ever learn. As I have shared before, most parenting experts agree that one of the most direct ways of modifying inappropriate behavior is to consistently give positive attention to the behavior that is more desirable.

Behavior Reinforcement Guide

Since too often parenting decisions are made by the seat of our pants (or sometimes by the seat of their pants!), it should come as a relief to know that here is an area for which you can actually prepare. Make lists of the positive behaviors that you want to remember to reward and acknowledge, as well as the negative acts that you want to avoid acknowledging. In that way, as you refer to this list each day, you will have a handy "Behavior Reinforcement Guide" to keep your parenting on the right path. With reminder list in hand, your decisions can more often be based on previously made, self-conscious choices that you believe will move your children further down the path of positive self-esteem and proper ethical behavior.

Exactly which kinds of rewards constitute the most effective ones to give to our children? This is a matter of great discussion and debate by child experts, with the result that there is little absolute agreement on what is truly best. Some claim that one should never reward a child for positive behavior by paying them (either with money, toys, or anything else). Others feel that for a reward to be effective in reinforcing positive behavior, it must be something that the child truly wants—whether a happy face sticker, 50 cents, a small toy, a candy bar, or a hug.

Parents who do pay their children for positive behavior often feel guilty about it. They believe that if they were really good and effective parents in the first place, their children would simply behave correctly due to their proper upbringing, and would have no need for external rewards and acknowledgments. I respectfully happen to disagree. My philosophy here, as with many important aspects of parenting can be summed up in the following *Dr. Reuben's Rule for Effective Parenting*. It goes like this: "Whatever works, works." If it works for you and isn't harmful to your children, by all means give it a try.

The truth is, all parents reward their children for positive behavior in one way or another. If you think about it for a moment, you will realize that all children act as they do because they are rewarded in some way. For some children the reward itself may be as simple as their parent's smile, while for others it may be that they are kicked out of the house and get to play outside with their friends, or maybe they are sent to their room. It's better to be assertive about your parenting rewards, set clear guidelines that everyone understands, and then follow through on acknowledgment of positive behavior at every opportunity, than to hold to a strict code that says "No external rewards," and ignore the fact that rewards are being given in one way or another anyway.

I believe that it doesn't particularly matter what the specific reward might be, and that what is effective for one parent and one child may not work for another. Either way the principle is the same—the more ways you can invent to reward desired behavior, the more likely it is that your children will internalize that behavior as they grow.

Parenting Is Art, Not Science

Rewards and punishments, how much to discipline, and when to give in to your children are the kinds of issues that never really get satisfactorily answered. The primary reason is that from year to year (and often day to day), situations change, your children change, you change, and the demands of the moment change. What might be appropriate at one given time in your life with your children, may seem inappropriate or inadequate or too strict, or not firm and consistent enough at a later time, or with a different child.

Learning to relax and not be in such a panic about your child-raising decisions will go a long way toward helping you to make the correct decisions. Once you have set relatively clear guidelines for yourself and communicated to your children your basic expectations regarding their behavior, the rest is art and not science. Obviously, this entire book has been written with the desire to give you a series of suggestions, guidelines, recommendations, and techniques for parenting in such a way as to encourage positive self-esteem and ethical behavior on the part of your children. At the same time, I realize that not every individual suggestion will match the specific needs of each parent or child. That is a decision that you will reach through a process of trial and error.

Discipline must be understood not merely as an issue of punishment or regaining control over a child or a situation, but as a learning opportunity for both parent and child. There are no perfect parents, and there are no magic formulas that will answer every question, address every issue, or respond to every situation that will arise between you and your children. The more you are open to a life-long process of experimentation, the less rigid you will become and the more flexible and tolerant will be your parenting style. This is an approach that I strongly recommend, even though it might be more emotionally satisfying for parents to simply have a "cookbook" approach to raising ethical children, where they can turn to the right chapter and verse to answer each and every ethical challenge. In my personal experience, that simply isn't the way that life works for anyone. I will give you a perfect example from my own parenting.

Dr. Don Dinkmeyer, in an article titled "Teaching Responsibility: Developing Personal Accountability Through Natural and Logical Consequences," wrote the following, quite reasonable explanation of the value of eschewing *punishment* in favor of *consequences* as a general rule for positive, ethical child raising:

> A child learns from consequences when his (sic) parents allow him to experience the results of his actions. Just as adults who have experienced the inconvenience of running out of gas are most apt to fill their tanks when the marker nears empty, the child who has experienced hunger because he forgot his lunch is more likely to remember to take the lunch bag from the refrigerator before leaving for school.

This concept is true in theory, and I also strongly urge parents to think not of punishments (which are always externally imposed), but of simply allowing their children to experience the consequences of their behavior (which are internally generated). However, I must admit that based upon my own adolescent daughter's behavior, it doesn't always work out exactly as you might expect in practice.

Gable had the bad habit of rushing out of the house in the morning on her way to school so quickly that she would either forget to take her lunch or forget to ask for money to buy her lunch. I kept telling her that it was her responsibility to see to it that she had either the lunch itself or the money, and that I wasn't going to remind her, or rescue her by bringing it to her if she forgot it, or frankly even worry much about it at all.

Unfortunately, instead of it becoming a lesson in the negative consequences of haste or lack of responsibility, it simply became a challenge to her creativity and ability to enlist the aid of friends and acquaintances in her weekly lunch treasure hunt. In fact, her survival skills were admirable, and she became quite adept at getting along just fine by borrowing lunch money from someone with a little extra, or sharing parts of various friends' lunches. The expected negative results and concomitant "lesson" in consequences and responsibility simply never materialized as I had expected. Instead, the lessons she learned were of a very different kind indeed. And, to add insult to injury, this was going on even as I was in the midst of writing this book! So much for parenting theory versus the surprises of reality which your child will bring into your life.

Art and the Element of Surprise

I tell this story because I think it reveals a very important lesson about rules and expectations when it comes to the art of parenting. You really never know for sure exactly how things will turn out. All you can do is the best you can. All you can be is the best example you can of the kind of adult and parent you would be proud to have your own children grow up to become, and the rest is out of your hands.

Certainly parenting involves skills that can be learned, practiced, deepened, and made to advance the process of encouraging your children to grow up to be emotionally healthy, fulfilled, highly functioning, responsible, ethical human beings. If I didn't wholeheartedly believe in that, I wouldn't have written this book. But, nevertheless, there is always that undeniable element of "art" in parenting, too. It is the element of surprise, the element of the unknown, the element that sometimes catches you off guard with as much delight as it does frustration, and reminds you that

human beings, even young ones, are complex, complicated, unpredictable and marvelously capricious beings,
who will surprise you again and again, sometimes turning
sure parenting disasters into remarkable successes.

Punishment versus Consequence

There are very important differences between the emotional experience of punishments versus that of consequences for your child. For example, *punishment* stresses
the power of individual authority (that of the parents); *consequences* reinforce the reality of natural order. *Punishment*
is inevitably personalized to the individual, implying a negative moral judgment (which may or may not actually be
true); *consequences* separate the action from the actor, and
are experienced as ultimately impersonal. *Punishment*
appears to be concerned primarily with past behavior, what
has already been done; *consequences* actually focus on present and even future behavior. *Punishment* tends to belittle
the child, communicating both disapproval and even dis-
respect; *consequences* can even take place in a supportive,
warm, friendly environment as they are natural, predictable, and usually inevitable. *Punishment* is an authori-
tarian demand for obedience; *consequences* reflect the
important element of choice.

Choice

Clearly, the key to the power and success of the consequences approach to ethical child raising is the issue of
choice. It is the fundamental acknowledgment of individual
free will, exercised by the mind and judgment of the child,
that empowers the child to feel that she or he ultimately
can gain mastery over her or his environment. Without
choice, without free will, without the ability to make

independent thoughtful decisions that carry inevitable consequences in their wake, our children are stripped of the power to exercise control over their environment, and are robbed of the possibility to make moral choices that strengthen their own sense of personal competence and positive self-esteem.

The Importance of Experiencing Consequences

Allowing your children to experience the consequences of their actions, rather than simply imposing artificial punishments, is really a way of demonstrating respect for your child. It is a method that communicates that you trust them to learn and grow from the unfolding experiences of their actions, mistakes, and choices.

Giving children the opportunity to make mistakes and live with the aftermath of those mistakes teaches them not only that every action in life does have a consequence, but that they are not so fragile that making mistakes or poor decisions will result in their entire world collapsing.

As the quotation at the beginning of this chapter states, even eight-year-old Carin understood the difference between punishments and rewards. When we were discussing the forms of parental discipline that she felt were most effective at her young age, without any prompting from me at all, she immediately said that it is much better for parents to allow their children to see what happens when they act in certain ways that are wrong, without jumping in to add punishments that only confuse the issue.

Punishments often get in the way of effective discipline with your children, because they distract both you and the children from the real issue—which is learning to live with the results of their own actions, and discovering that every action in life does have its own special consequence.

When I asked Carin why she thought that "discipline by consequences" was a better way for parents to raise their children than "discipline by punishment," she didn't say what I expected, namely, that no kid likes to be punished. Instead, she wisely pointed out that the main advantage of experiencing consequences over punishments is that "a punishment is something that a parent does to you; a consequence is something that you do to yourself."

In other words, Carin (and I believe most children in their hearts) easily understood that by imposing external punishments on her instead of allowing the natural consequences of her actions to provide the lesson, her parents would actually be robbing her of the opportunity to experience the full impact of what personal responsibility for her actions is all about.

Doing the Best You Can

Even with the very best of intentions, as a parent with a heart full of love, caring, nurturing, and support for your children, ultimately all you can do is the best you can. The basic keys to effective discipline are not that difficult to understand, but they are hard to follow through with consistently day after day.

The goal of effective ethical parenting is to create an environment in your home in which your children understand the behavior expected of them, and where with as much consistency as possible, you have clearly articulated your goals and expectations for your children regarding how they act with you and other adults, with their peers, and in the world in general.

The goal is to nurture a sense of self-mastery in your children, to empower them to make the often difficult and even painful decisions that all human beings make in their daily lives, and to know that they can live with the consequences of their actions, even when they aren't particularly pleasant or easy.

All we can really expect from ourselves is that we do the best we can, with the best of intentions. Don't be too hard on yourself. Treat yourself with care and kindness, and know that if you are reading books like this, if you are doing your best to create a warm, accepting, flexible, yet consistent, ethical climate within your home, your children will most likely turn out just fine.

Doing the best you can *is* the best you can do. Take it one day at a time, one experience at a time, and ideally find or create a support group of other parents with whom you can share experiences, frustrations, ideas, and successes. This is one of the best ways to reinforce your own sense of self-worth as a parent. Being part of a parenting group that shares experiences and gives each other advice and feedback can provide you with ongoing support and encouragement to help you through the rough days, and give you a place to receive acknowledgement and joy in moments of success and satisfaction.

In the next chapter we will look at the origins of our personal ethical values, and the values that have formed the foundation of Western ethics for the past 4,000 years. We will share the ethical imperatives that have naturally flowed from both Judaism and Christianity, and which form the basis of the expectations for ethical behavior that we strive to pass on to our children.

Four

Judeo–Christian Ethics: The Roots of Our Values

Train up a child in the way that he should go, and even when he is old he will not depart from it.

Proverbs 22:6

This book and its underlying philosophy of ethical child raising, are both clearly grounded in my own strong religious upbringing. My belief in the importance of establishing within your children a clear sense of right and wrong is a direct result of being grounded in what has come to be called *ethical monotheism*.

Ethical monotheism is an idea that Judaism first introduced to the Western world through the teachings of the prophets and sages of the Bible—initially through those books that Christians came to call the "Old Testament." It is within the pages of the Bible that we first encounter the notion that the world was created by a transcendent Source of Life. This Power, which for the past few thousand years we have called "God," is both beyond the full understanding of human beings, and yet clearly the ultimate source of the ethics, morality, and values that we are to help bring into being within our daily lives.

This view of the world, grounded in what is generally understood to be the foundation of Judeo–Christian ethics, leads me to believe that the world as we know it was created to be inhabited by human beings for the purpose of bringing holiness, goodness, justice, compassion, and joy into our lives.

I believe that the foundation of our ethical and moral system rests with a divine Source or Power in the universe that is the ground of all ethical being. In fact, I believe that it is this recognition that there is a moral authority in the universe whose ethical standards of behavior we aspire to emulate that gives us the ability to assert that some behavior is right and some behavior is simply wrong, regardless of individual opinion or upbringing.

Our commitment to standards and expectations of ethical behavior that we believe are universal rests on our denial of moral relativism, no matter how "modern," or

attractive that notion may seem to our contemporary, egal-
itarian, universal-minded sensibilities.

This book is grounded on a view of the universe that
teaches that "Thou shall not murder" is not merely my personal feeling or belief system. It is based on the assumption
that there is an ethical standard to which all human beings
must be held if the world itself is to survive. The idea that
there is an identifiable, universally recognized standard of
ethics in the religious realm found its moral echo in the
secular world during the famous trials at Nuremberg following the Holocaust of World War II. It was there, during
the trials of Nazi war criminals on charges of "crimes
against humanity," that "merely following orders" ceased
for all time to be a sufficient defense for unethical, brutal
behavior.

Since I continue to believe that Western civilization is
based on this universally acknowledged Judeo–Christian
ethical foundation, I also believe that it is our responsibility
as parents to pass on the best of that ethical tradition to our
children. Giving them clear messages regarding the ethical
implications of the choices that they make each day, and
helping them to understand that every decision they make
becomes part and parcel of forming the very essence of
their moral character are the most challenging and important jobs we will ever have.

I believe that it is much easier to raise ethical children
when you are personally grounded in the ethical principles
of monotheism, and have the bedrock of the Judeo–Christian ideals of ethical behavior to use as your guideposts.
That is why in this chapter I will call your attention to the
Ten Commandments and several other key ethical ideas
from the Biblical tradition which can serve as key examples
of how you can use the ethical traditions of Western spiritual civilization to serve your goal of raising ethical children.

The Golden Rule

One of the best known of all ethical standards of behavior started with a rabbi named Hillel about 2,000 years ago in the land of Israel. There is a famous story told of a pagan who came to the great Hillel and said he would become a Jew if Hillel could teach him the entire Torah (specifically the five books of Moses, but also a term used to refer to Jewish teachings in general), while standing on one foot.

Rather than become annoyed with what was probably meant as ridicule, Hillel is said to have calmly and lovingly replied, "What is hateful to you, do not do unto your neighbor: this is the entire Torah. All the rest is commentary—now go and study it."

Many of you may be more familiar with this phrase as it was retold by Hillel's most famous student, who is quoted in the New Testament book of Matthew as saying, "Do unto others as you would have others do unto you." This is the famous "Golden Rule" of Jesus, who scholars think probably studied under Hillel, since many of the aphorisms attributed to him in the Gospels of the New Testament are actually beautiful reformulations of Hillel's own teachings.

"What is hateful to you, do not do unto your neighbor" is a formula for loving your neighbor as yourself. It is possibly an even more inclusive statement than the Golden Rule version, since it is directed at the other and not at the self. Avoiding acting in any way that you would find unacceptable is the simplest way possible to establish a foolproof system of proper ethical behavior.

Whether it is fulfilled in the original or in the form of the famous Golden Rule, acting in such a way that you "Do unto others as you would have them do unto you" would surely result in a world that holds itself to a much higher ethical standard than most of us seem to experience at the moment. That is our ultimate parenting goal—to inspire our children with the desire to create a world that reflects this fundamental ethical principle in every realm of society. Since the Western world is founded primarily on the ethical principles espoused in the teachings of Judaism and Christianity, they can serve as useful tools in the ethical training of our children, regardless of the particular religious heritage we might individually espouse.

The "How Would I Like It?" Rule

For example, how might you translate Hillel's rule for a child? You can tell your child that the easiest test to apply to her own behavior in almost any circumstance is the "How would I like it if the situation were reversed?" test.

Whenever she has any question whatsoever concerning the appropriateness of her behavior, all she has to do is imagine that the tables were turned, with the other person acting toward her as she is toward them. If that would be OK with her, then her behavior is probably OK as well. If she would not like it, then it's a pretty good bet that she shouldn't be doing it to anyone else either.

"What is hateful to you do not do unto your neighbor" is another ethical standard by which we can measure how well we are living out what is clearly one of the most important ethical ideas ever taught—"Love your neighbor as yourself." If we are behaving in a way that is consistent with Hillel's famous admonition of the Golden Rule, then we can be fairly certain that we are doing a passable job of living the commandment to love our neighbor as ourselves in our daily lives.

If you use these rules to set guidelines and standards for your children, you will be passing on to them the most important ideals and values that have grown out of the thousands of years of Judeo-Christian ethics, history, and culture. By laying this crucial ethical foundation for them early in their lives, you will have gone a long way toward fulfilling your essential parental obligation of raising your children to be caring, compassionate, ethical, loving human beings.

The Primary Goal of Humanity

Another fundamental ethical principle that is important to teach to your children was developed by the religious leaders and great sages of the Judeo–Christian tradition many hundreds of years ago. It is reflected in a specific spiritual understanding of the role of humanity on earth.

What, according to these teachers, is the primary goal of humanity? It is to join with God as partners in completing the work of creation. In the Western religious tradition, we teach that "God" is the term we use to refer to that Power that is the source of creation in the universe. That same Power which animated all life from the beginning of time and continues to renew creation on a daily basis, according to Judeo–Christian tradition, needs us human beings to be partners in finishing Its work.

The Challenge of "Healing the World"

Our job is what my tradition calls *Tikun Olam*. Tikun Olam literally means "healing the world." We are challenged with the task of repairing this broken world of ours (and certainly no one would argue that it is whole), and bringing it ever closer to the ultimate goal of wholeness and peace.

Embracing as our own the challenge of healing the world means seeing our primary task as human beings as doing whatever we can in our lifetime to bring a sense of completeness and fulfillment into the world around us. We are to repair the broken fragments of the world in which we live—heal the shattered lives around us; bring comfort to the sick at heart; bring healing to the sick of body; bring shelter to the homeless; bring food to the starving; bring clothes to the ragged; bring hope to those in despair.

Healing the world is a life-long task for all of us. It is the ultimate challenge of ethical parenting—to inspire our children to see the world as if they too are responsible for the way it all turns out. This only happens when you teach them to see themselves as intimately connected to other human beings as an integral part of the greater social fabric of life. The task becomes even more complex when you realize that at the same time they must feel a deep connection with all other human beings, they must also believe in the "power of one." They must feel deep within their innermost being that the most important job, the most crucial challenge that any of us face, is in being the best *us* that we can be.

Being the Best "Us" We Can Be

Without question, one of the greatest realizations that any child can be blessed with, is that of all the billions of human beings on earth, *she* is one of a kind. There never has been, in all the millions of years of the world's history, and there never will be in the future, another human being exactly like her. She is unique, the only "her" that will ever be, and as such her task while she is on this beautiful planet, is to simply be the best "her" she can possibly be.

Too often our children shed tears of grief, longing to be someone else, wondering why they aren't the girl down the block who always seems so popular, or the boy next door who is star quarterback on the football team, or the kid in their class who always gets the A's on every test, and so on, and so on. They struggle to be someone else, never realizing that try as they might they will never be able to be better than the original, even if the original person isn't that special to begin with.

At the same time, no matter how hard someone else may try to be like them, others will never do it as well—no matter what. That is why being yourself, just being the best that you can possibly be, is the most important challenge in life. For you are the only one who can do it!

Successful ethical parenting involves communicating to your children that they can make a difference in the world. It requires that they discover with your help, that even with all the problems that afflict our world, with all the pain and suffering, all the sorrow and grief, all the struggles and frustrations, *they* have the power to bring more light, joy, and love into even the darkest corner.

Teaching the Meaning of Life

People don't have to be famous inventors, scientists, athletes, entertainers, or political figures to accomplish the most important things in life. After all, your job is to teach your children that the most important things in life aren't things at all. They are found in the quiet moments of caring and love that pass between lovers, friends, parents and children, and teachers and students.

Touching the world, healing the world, is possible for everyone, and it is probably the most important reason for being alive. In the Judeo–Christian tradition rightly understood, the meaning of life is found in reaching out to others. Jews and Christians alike reject the isolation of living for oneself alone, in favor of the responsibilities that come with being part of a community, a people, and a family.

The Biblical prophecy of Judaism commands, "Let justice well up as waters and righteousness like a mighty stream" (Amos 5:24), and the teachings of Jesus echo "Blessed are those who hunger and thirst for righteousness, for they shall be satisfied. Blessed are the merciful, for they shall obtain mercy" (Matthew 5:6–7). Both traditions teach the importance of bringing justice and compassion into the world, and can serve as constant reminders that thousands of years of history, traditions, and evolving ethical standards underlie the challenge we have taken up of passing these values along to the next generation.

For our children to embrace the Judeo–Christian challenge to be active participants in healing the world, means they need to experience their lives as connected to the lives of all other human beings. It essentially means feeling responsible for the quality of life on our planet—the quality of the air we breathe, the water we drink, the food we eat, the well-being of our society as a whole, and the fate of humanity on this tiny, fragile, wonderful planet.

Teaching that responsibility to your children is both challenging and exciting. More often than not, it takes place in the simple gestures and ordinary moments of our lives. Our challenge is to teach our children that when they look back on their lives, they will realize that the most important things were not written large in the bold print of headlines—they were found in the small print of their everyday encounters with each human being who crossed their path, and whose lives they touched.

An Ethical Homework Assignment

To teach your children that it is our responsibility together to do whatever we can to create a world that nurtures, supports, and sustains everyone with dignity, compassion, and caring requires that you identify the same type of concrete behavior necessary to teach the idea of loving your neighbor as yourself.

For example, we engage in healing the world each time we do our part to right a wrong, or bring more justice, hope, or love into the lives of others. I always encourage parents to take this on as a concrete assignment that they can do with their children. The more you can focus together on specific behaviors that they can do that will have an impact on the world around them, the more you will help them to feel more powerful and competent as ethical human beings.

One of the simplest methods of fulfilling this "ethical homework assignment" is to sit down with your children and ask them, "What do you think is wrong with the world?" Then as they share their ideas, list all the things they come up with on a piece of paper.

After your list is done (you can always go back and add to it later), write each entry on the top of a single page of paper. Next have a family "brainstorming" session with parents and children both participating in which you take one problem at a time and think of as many different and creative ideas as you can for fixing it. The more inventive and unusual the better, for it helps all of you to break out of the easy-to-think-of, ordinary solutions to the important issues that inevitably emerge.

Go through as many problems as you can, listing things that might be done to ease the problem by kids, adults, schools, government, religious or civic groups, neighborhoods, sports teams, families, girls, boys, college students, professors, parent–teacher associations, or anyone else you might think of. When your list is done (or you simply want a break from listing solutions), sit down as a family and pick *one* approach with which to begin. This will constitute your first family Healing the World Pledge.

The Family Healing the World Pledge

Take a new piece of paper and write on the top "THE FAMILY HEALING THE WORLD PLEDGE." Underneath the heading, write a sentence that describes what you are pledging to do as a family first in order to address the problem that you have selected. Then have each family member sign the pledge, and agree upon a timetable for implementing your plan. This can also be done as individual pledges, but the important thing is to pick something concrete that you are actually able to accomplish.

If you make this an on-going family activity, you can involve children of any age in the process of making the world better. For example, you might decide that you want to help the environment suffer less from the greenhouse effect, and your first activity might be a pledge to plant a tree for every member of your family. Children of all ages can participate in the variety of activities necessary to fulfill this pledge, including choosing the kind of tree, finding a location, getting the necessary tools, the dirt, and the tree itself, and then helping with the actual planting. Your job as parent–teacher is to join with your children in the activity while pointing out that what they are doing is fulfilling an important ethical, religious value, called "Healing the World."

Another example might be to address some of the problems associated with the thousands of homeless children in our society. You might make your family Healing the World Pledge to collect clothing from your neighbors and bring it to a shelter in your community that helps such families in need. This would allow all your children who can understand the concept to go into their own closets to find clothes, toys, or blankets to share with the homeless children.

A Birthday to Remember

Another wonderful project that one child I know chose to do was to turn her own birthday into an opportunity to bring joy, laughter, and love into the lives of homeless children and their families. Instead of having a birthday party for herself, she got her entire family to cook food, bake cakes and cookies, and create decorations for a birthday party, which they then delivered in person to a local family shelter. This young child of twelve experienced the ultimate birthday gift of truly feeling the joy that comes with touching the lives of others in a meaningful way, by sharing her own birthday party with a group of homeless children.

It is difficult for most of us to understand just how powerful such an experience can be for a young child. This little girl was sensitive enough to realize how fortunate she was in her life. She understood that she was blessed with a life filled with the comforts of home that most of us take for granted. She had plenty of food, lovely clothing, more toys and games than she could ever use, the love of family and friends that surrounded her, and the realization that there were other children who went to bed each night hungry, not knowing where they would sleep or even whether their parents would be able to keep their family together.

Transforming Lives

Obviously, this was a young child of unusual sensitivity and compassion. But these feelings didn't spring suddenly out of the blue. They were the result of growing up in a family with parents who consistently expressed a conviction that all people were ultimately responsible for the welfare of one another in a society. She had wonderful role models, and in wanting to emulate the best that she saw in her parents, she came up with this beautiful and creative way of transforming what would otherwise have been a self-indulgent birthday into an opportunity for adding greater meaning and fulfillment into the lives of others.

The wonderful lesson in all of this for the child was that in sharing her own good fortune with others, in transforming their lives, she also transformed her own. She learned firsthand the truth of the cliché that it is better to give than to receive, for she experienced an unbelievable sense of joy and satisfaction in expanding her birthday celebration to include so many others who were in need.

Stressing Ethical Actions

The opportunities for involving your children and your entire family in projects that will bring hope and help to the lives of others while adding satisfaction and fulfillment to your own lives are endless. The problems of homelessness will be with us for a long time, and with a little creative thinking I am certain that you can come up with your own caring projects to serve as examples of ethical social action for your children.

Family projects that stress ethical action toward others do not have to be elaborate, or exotic, or extravagant. Even the simplest acts, when taken within a context of ethical concern for making the world a little better for our having been around, can have a powerful and lasting impact upon your children. You might have your entire family collect cans of food, or write letters to local city officials asking them to help in organizing a shelter for homeless families if one doesn't already exist. Sit down as a family and write a "letter to the editor" of your local newspaper encouraging others to donate food, clothing, or financial contributions to the local homeless relief agencies within your community.

One of your children might just turn out like fourteen-year-old Trevor, who decided one day that his family should make sandwiches and other portable food, and drive their car around Philadelphia to deliver food to the homeless who lived on the streets in his community. His personal act of healing the world soon involved his entire family, neighborhood, city, and country when he was honored by then President Ronald Reagan for starting what became a community-wide program for feeding the homeless.

The possibilities are virtually endless. All it takes is for you to embrace healing the world as a value worth teaching your children, and the willingness to participate with them in activities that bring it to life.

Ultimately, the key to raising ethical children who are connected to the Judeo–Christian roots of our values, is to remember that children learn what they live. Create as many opportunities as you can to weave ethical action into the everyday fabric of your family's life. In that way your children will grow up knowing that their challenge as human beings is to do their part to repair the broken fragments of our troubled world, and that what they do and who they are do make a difference after all.

What Does Holiness Really Mean?

If you ever want to glance through the Bible in search of pearls of ethical wisdom, start with Chapter 19 of the book of Leviticus. Jewish tradition called it the "Holiness Code" because it contains the most concise prescription ever written for how to create a society that reflects the original Judeo–Christian ideal of holiness.

In Leviticus, to be "holy" means to act in such a way as to bring our highest and noblest ideals and values into play in our everyday lives. It is not a prescription for mystic meditation, or secluding oneself away from the world; it is rather a command to clothe the naked, house the homeless, care for the elderly and frail, treat people with dignity, compassion, and justice. That's holiness for the Biblical writer, and our task as parents is to utilize this wisdom from ancient Biblical texts to inspire our own children to understand that they, too, can bring ethical holiness into their lives, at any age.

Our Western religious tradition sees holiness as something reflected in the actions of human beings. We embody holiness when we fulfill the best and noblest that lies within us.

Chapter 19 of Leviticus contains a fabulous list of the various responsibilities we have toward other human beings, such that if we each acted on these "commandments" and taught them to our children, the world would be the kind of place in which we all dream of living.

In fact, Chapter 19 contains one of the single most important religious ideas ever expressed. It is found in the middle of verse 18, and I am sure you already know it, since it is without doubt one of the most famous verses in all the Bible. It reads simply, " . . . YOU SHALL LOVE YOUR NEIGHBOR AS YOURSELF."

Love your neighbor as yourself. Sounds fairly simple, yet it contains one of the most sophisticated notions in all of Biblical ethics. The obvious meaning of the text seems to simply command us to extend love to our neighbors. But the understated zinger in these simple five words is that to love your neighbor as yourself, first *you have to love yourself.*

Have you ever been on an airplane and listened as the flight attendant ran through the emergency procedures before the flight? If so, recall that he or she explained that in the event of a sudden unexpected loss of cabin pressure oxygen masks would drop down from the ceiling in front of your seat. The attendant then said, "If you are traveling with small children, place the oxygen mask on *yourself first,* then put the masks on your children."

What, you might ask, do oxygen masks on airplanes have to do with Biblical ethics? Well, just as you must put the mask on yourself first, before you are fit to effectively take care of anyone else in an airplane emergency, so too before you are fit to demonstrate love for another human being, you must be able to extend love to yourself.

"Loving another as yourself" by definition implies that you love yourself. Every psychologist and psychiatrist I have ever spoken with has affirmed the fact that individuals who are incapable of loving themselves, of nurturing feelings of positive self-worth and value, are equally incapable of truly expressing love for anyone else.

Love Others, Love Yourself

What then are the implications for child raising contained in the "Love your neighbor as yourself" idea? First, it is important for you to realize as a parent that teaching your children to love themselves does not imply that they will be selfish, egotistical, self-centered, ill-mannered, spoiled, or demanding. All of these come from overindulgence of their whims or desires, spoiling your children by withholding the kind of structure, discipline, and limits that children desperately need.

To grow up as fully functioning, emotionally mature adults, your children need the strong foundation of self-love which only you can provide. One of the great paradoxes of raising emotionally healthy children, is that a significant part of their self-love will grow directly out of experiences in which they see themselves as expressing love for others. In fact, as odd as it may seem at first, it is often primarily through such experiences of loving others in concrete, identifiable ways, that we reinforce our own self-worth and value as caring human beings. Let us look at some specific examples of just how this process works.

Loving Your Neighbor in Action

First, you might take your children with you to volunteer at a local soup kitchen or homeless shelter. At almost any age, children have a natural compassion for others (especially other children) who are in need. Children have a built-in sense of fairness and justice. As any parent will tell you, one of the most frequently heard complaints from our children are the three little words, "It's not fair!"

Kids want life to be fair, and are constantly frustrated by the discovery that it isn't. Obviously, many adults feel exactly the same way, share the same frustrations and commit themselves to various forms of social action and community involvement in an attempt at creating a society which is in fact more fair, more just, and more equitable.

So kids know what you are talking about when you speak of fairness. They know that it isn't fair for little kids to be homeless, and it isn't fair for little kids to be hungry. It isn't fair for little kids to go without nice clothes, or things to play with, or friends. The chances are very good that you will constantly be surprised by the depth of passion with which your children sincerely care about the plight of others. This is particularly surprising to many parents, since childhood is most often typified by an incredible self-indulgence, self-centeredness, self-focus on the part of children. Learning to live with and even celebrate the ambiguities and paradoxes of our children, is, after all, one of the great challenges of parenting in a modern world.

Children Learn What They Live

Children learn what they live, plain and simple. There are few claims in life more devastating than that leveled at parents, teachers, or religious leaders that we teach one standard, and live another. Children have an aggravating habit of being able to spot the truth every time. You just can't fool them. If you want to teach your children that to be a good ethical human being you must love others and show them compassion, caring, and concern, you must live those values yourself.

So after all this, how do you teach the concept "love your neighbor" to your children? It isn't through trying to nurture warm and loving *feelings* or lofty and grandiose *thoughts* about how wonderful your neighbors might be. It is, rather, directly reflected in the *actions* you take which demonstrate your compassion for others. In fact, it's about action and not thoughts or feelings at all. No one really knows what goes on in anyone else's mind and heart. Even your children can never really tell how you (or anyone else) truly feels about others. What they can know from direct experience is what you do about the world around you.

I realize that it is often difficult for parents to truly accept the awesome responsibility that they have brought upon themselves by becoming parents. You have made yourself responsible not only for the physical and emotional nurturing of your children, but for providing them with the most positive role model that you can be. Your children will emulate what you do, and won't pay much attention to what you say (in case you haven't noticed by now) unless it is consistent with your own behavior.

As the primary role model for your children, you will determine what they integrate into the emotional center of their lives as right or wrong, important or unimportant, necessary or useless, functional or dysfunctional, particularly when it comes to issues of how they perceive and treat other people.

In the end, our children will learn that one of the most important of all religious values is "Love your neighbor as yourself," only to the degree that we ourselves demonstrate what such loving behavior is all about.

Follow the Ten Commandments

If you ask most people who have grown up in the Western world to identify the foundation of their ethics, they will probably point to the Ten Commandments. That they exist as the cornerstone of Western morality is, of course, much more widely remembered than are the commandments themselves. Try to name all of them right now, and you will probably only remember a few. Don't be upset, since when first asked, most people remember only "Don't kill" (which is actually "Don't murder"), "Don't commit adultery," and "Don't steal."

Yet, it is these Ten Commandments which are the most often quoted foundation upon which all subsequent ethics are based. The Ten Commandments have continued to inspire volumes of ethical dissertations, study, commentary, and exhortation throughout the thousands of years that they have influenced Western civilization. For your purposes in raising ethical children, they can serve as excellent guidelines for a basic list of universal ethical values as well.

The Ten Commandments Themselves

Let's look at the Ten Commandments and remind ourselves of what they teach. The following is the list as presented in Exodus 20:2–14 (a slightly different version is presented in Deuteronomy 5:6–18):

1. I am your God who brought you out of the land of Egypt, out of the house of bondage.

2. You shall have no other Gods besides me.

3. You shall not use God's name in vain.

4. Remember the Sabbath day to make it holy.

5. Honor your father and mother.

6. You shall not murder.

7. You shall not commit adultery.

8. You shall not steal.

9. You shall not bear false witness against your neighbor.

10. You shall not covet your neighbor's house, your neighbor's wife . . . or anything that is your neighbor's.

The First Commandment

OK, now that you have reviewed the commandments themselves, you may have a question about why the first one is included in such a list in the first place. It certainly doesn't seem to "command" us to do anything particular at all. In fact, many commentators throughout the centuries have asked exactly the same question, and arrived at different answers.

Most religious teachers have understood the first statement ("I am your God . . .) as an indirect command to believe in God. I see it as the quintessential challenge regarding belief in God, in a "higher power," in the reality of an Ultimate Source of creation because it doesn't actually say anything about belief at all! It forces us to *imply* the existence of a power greater than human beings (which in English we call by the name "God"), by simply pointing to the single most powerful collective *experience* first shared by the Jewish people—who brought the world this God idea in the first place—namely, their liberation from over 400 years of slavery in Egypt.

God Is the Power That Inspires Freedom

Within Jewish theology, the most compelling evidence for the reality of God's presence in the universe lies in the very reality of human history itself. The reality of history is that Jews were slaves in Egypt, and at a particular moment in history, they walked to freedom. As a result of this historical reality, the Jewish tradition has celebrated freedom ever since, as the most fundamental "God-given" state of humanity. Just as Jews experienced what it was to be enslaved and then go free, so too they project the power of liberation from all bondage as one of the primary ways we experience the presence of God in the universe. Since almost all people and cultures have experienced slavery, oppression, bondage, and liberation, this association of freedom with godliness becomes a universal message of Western religious ethics.

That is why the Ten Commandments begin with the simple reminder that what we call God is found in that power that transforms our lives from that of slaves to that of free human beings. The First Commandment is really an exhortation to insist on freedom for everyone, to see freedom as the inalienable right of all people, and to recognize in that undying spark of freedom that burns in the breast of every human being, no matter what religion, no matter what race, no matter in what country they live, the spark of godliness that can never be dampened.

The genius of the Judeo–Christian ethical gift to Western civilization is that our understanding of God is based on direct experience, and not only on blind faith. You don't have to teach your children to suspend their understanding of how the universe actually works, but rather to look to the very mystery of the unfolding of nature, the intricacy of the human body, the inexplicable perfection of the stars and planets as they move in their orbits, the indomitable will of the human soul to discover concrete reflections of the divine presence in the world around us.

That is why the First Commandment begins as it does. It establishes a kind of experiential credibility for the God who according to Judeo–Christian tradition is the power responsible for all the following commandments as well. It is as if the people were to ask, "What is the source of these universal ethical laws, and why should we follow them?" The answer comes in the First Commandment, as they recognize that the same transcendent power that inspired them to break the bonds of their slavery and walk to freedom is the source of all universal ethics and morality, as reflected in the commandments that follow.

Ethical Behavior Is an Outgrowth of Humility

How do you teach this idea to your children? It starts with the willingness to point to the everyday miracles of life as evidence that the world is governed by powers and laws that transcend human invention and design. To recognize that we are not the end all and be all of life—that there are forces in the universe much greater than us that we can use as sources of inspiration and awe—is the first step to developing a spiritual approach to living an ethical life.

It is equally important for children to grow up with an appropriate sense of their place in the universe, by reducing their natural tendency to unbridled arrogance and developing an understanding of the importance of humility. Ethical behavior is the result not only of training the everyday actions of your children by constant direction and feedback. It also must come from a deeper sense of being connected to all life, responsible for the quality of the society in which we live, and humbled by the realization that we are but a tiny drop in the vast sea of the cosmos.

Take your children outside away from the bright city lights on a clear night, and allow them to watch the stars. They can't help but be awed by the enormity of it all, the magnificence of the universe in which we live and be reminded of their own smallness. Show them pictures of the earth taken from the moon. Ask them to point to the boundaries that divide one country from the next, and join in their "aha!" when they realize that there *aren't* such boundaries except as we human beings have artificially created them. That is a primary lesson in the oneness of humanity, of the fact that there is more that unites us than there is that divides us, except as human beings out of their own fears and insecurities have brought them into being.

God Is Not a Being Who Lives in the Sky

All this comes from the First Commandment. It flows from the recognition that you can teach your children to see God reflected in the actual experiences of human beings, the beauty of a flower, the inspiration of love, the strength of courage, the tenderness of compassion, and as the first commandment reminds us, the act of personal freedom and liberation as well.

Just look at all that has taken place throughout Eastern Europe, Africa, and the Soviet Union over the past decade, and it will be obvious why this first commandment has retained its power and relevance throughout the centuries. The First Commandment then is really, "Teach your children that freedom is the inalienable divine right of every human being."

The Second Commandment—Avoid Idolatry

The Second Commandment, "You shall have no other Gods besides me," is a lesson in the importance of preventing idolatries of all kinds. In today's world in particular, our children are in danger of falling prey to the latest fads; the latest drugs; the latest thrills; the latest pop sensations, cult figures, and pseudo-religions.

"Idolatry" does not necessarily refer only to the worship of other religions or the statues and idols that dotted the ancient Middle East. For us, today, it can refer to anything that assumes primary importance in our lives in a way that somehow diminishes the important ethical values which our Judeo–Christian heritage teaches are the foundation of our moral existence. It is just such idolatries that we all want to teach our children to avoid.

For example, when we fall prey to addictions of all types, whether drugs, alcohol, food, gambling, or the host of other destructive compulsions to which our addictive personalities might succumb, we have effectively elevated these addictions to the level of idolatry. They become the "gods" we worship, the motivations for our actions and thoughts, the driving force that runs our daily lives.

It is precisely against such idolatries that the Second Commandment is warning. If it were being written today, it would cry, "Stay clean, stay sober, stay healthy, take care of your body, your spirit, your mind; and fill your thoughts with positive, loving, nurturing, life-affirming ideas every day." As parents, these are among our greatest fears—that our children will succumb to the temptations that these addictions represent. That is one of the reasons why a thorough grounding in the true meaning of the Ten Commandments today can help give us guidelines with which to direct our children away from such self-destructive behavior.

The Idolatry of Excess

The decade of the 1980s became known as the decade of greed—the "me" decade. The greed that fueled the scandals of Wall Street, Iran-Contra, and failing savings and loans was simply another form of idolatry that the Second Commandment warns against. Money must be a means to an end, not an end in itself. The Bible doesn't teach us that money is the root of all evil, only that the *pursuit* of money can lead us astray, blind us to the ultimate values that are truly important in our lives, and allow us to cause grief, pain, and suffering to everyone around us.

The idolatry that greed represents also finds expression in the all too pervasive self-indulgence that has become commonplace in modern society. Too many people act as if excess were the same as excellence, as if the more we consume the more we demonstrate our value as human beings.

The Second Commandment is a reminder that all such excesses, whether in the form of money, things, drugs, or celebrity worship, diminish our children's ability to live their lives according to the values that ennoble, uplift, and inspire them and bring the world closer to the kind of place we dream it can become.

Teaching by Doing

You teach the lessons of the Second Commandment to your children, first by supporting and participating in the programs that already exist in your community to combat drugs, alcohol, and the like in kids. Most importantly, the primary way you teach these values to your children is by living them yourself. If you take drugs, drink alcohol every day, talk mostly about how much money you will be or are making, what clubs you can belong to, or act as if the acquisition of things is the ultimate goal of life, then you are passing those idolatries on to your children as well.

Instead, create projects with your children where the goal is to identify the important things of life. Have everyone in your family write down the three most important things in your home to them, and compare notes. Ask what would happen if there were a fire and those things were destroyed? How crucial are they really to the everyday lives of your family? If you never had them again, how would it affect your lives?

Now write down (or share verbally with kids who are too young to write comfortably) the three most important things in your life that aren't things (people, relationships, feelings, personality traits, abilities, and so on). Imagine how different your lives would be if these were missing, and it becomes obvious immediately where your true values lie. Even small children will understand that it is more important to have the love of parents and siblings, and the freedom to live life as they choose than to have the latest Nintendo game or doll that turns into a flying machine.

The Third Commandment—Integrity

The Third Commandment has to do with teaching integrity. It is usually mistranslated and misunderstood to mean that one shouldn't swear (as in "goddamn") or say the word God when you don't really mean it in a religious sense. The real meaning of "You shall not use God's name in vain" refers to an ancient practice of calling upon one's ultimate authority (in this case God) when making a vow or a pledge. It is similar to the practice today of "swearing in" by raising your right hand in a courtroom and promising ("so help me God") to tell the truth in what you are about to say.

If you promise to tell the truth, and convince others that it really is the truth, by using God as a kind of spiritual collateral when in fact you are lying, it degrades the image of God in the eyes of the world.

The purpose of all this is really to teach a lesson in how important it is to be someone that others can count on. Integrity in life is one of the most important attributes that any human being can have. It means that when you say you will do something, others can count on the fact that it will happen because you said it will. It means that your "yes" is a yes, and your "no" is a no.

That is why included as one of the Ten Commandments is this warning not to use the name of God frivolously in making promises. In this sense, "God" is used to represent the highest and most important values that you embrace. If you are willing to denigrate even the most important values in your life by using them to lie to others, then you are obviously not worthy of anyone's trust ever.

Demonstrating Integrity

You teach your children integrity by insisting that they keep their word. Again (as I will repeat throughout this book), children learn what they live, primarily from the living examples that you present them. You carry the most important responsibility for demonstrating to your children what integrity means. They must experience it first-hand by watching you, learning from how you act, seeing how you treat others, and realizing that you and your word can be counted on. That is the single most important way you teach integrity to another—by demonstrating it your-self.

You can also be aware of the inevitable times when your children (and you) are let down by others who fall short of keeping their word. Point out how disappointed you are, how upsetting it is to live in a world in which you can't count on someone to do what they say, and how much you respect and admire those people in your life who do have integrity.

There will be ample opportunities to demonstrate to your children the difference between integrity and its absence. Praise them every time they follow through on a promise, whether it's to go to bed at a particular time, return in time for dinner, clean up their room, do the dishes, finish their homework before watching television, or whatever. The specific example makes no difference at all. The point to be made is that you are proud of them every time they demonstrate integrity and trustworthiness. It is up to you to reinforce time and again how singly important this quality is to you, and how crucial it is to making the world a better place in which to live.

The Fourth Commandment—Make Life Holy

The Fourth Commandment is a reminder that we have the power to make life holy, special, and extraordinary. The Fourth Commandment can be used as a tool to teach your children about the importance of taking control of that which is in their power, and not allowing outside forces to dictate the quality of their lives.

The "Sabbath" can be a metaphor for achieving mastery over our lives, creating time to contemplate who we are, where we are going, what our goals are in life, and the kind of people we wish to become. It is a symbol of consciousness, for it reminds us that unlike animals who have no choice but to act in accordance with preordained instincts, we human beings have the power to write our own life stories, to chart our own courses, to make conscious choices concerning just about everything that is important in our lives.

The best way to teach these values to your children is to guide them in making intelligent choices at the different stages of their lives. Begin when they are young by giving them alternatives from which to choose, and praising them whenever they make positive, constructive choices.

As they get older, help them by creating a structure that allows for both work and play, school and extracurricular activities, while pointing out the importance of having this balance in their lives. It is also important for them to realize that they have the ability to make life holy, special, or sacred. When they set aside time to view a spectacular sunset, give of themselves to help another by tutoring them, or extend a hand when needed to lighten another's load, these are examples of what holiness is all about.

Mitzvah Framing

In a sense ethical parenting is a function of what I call "mitzvah framing." A *mitzvah* in traditional Jewish language is the equivalent of a commandment. As I use it, it represents any ethical act or religious obligation. It is "doing the right thing" in a given circumstance, and can inevitably be linked to one of these important ethical values that we are discussing.

"Mitzvah" framing means taking the activities, experiences, and opportunities that you find in your life and the lives of your children and placing an ethical concept, idea, or commandment around them like a frame. It means pausing when you see your child help another; to say to your child, "I'm proud of you when you do a caring act like that," "I love seeing you demonstrating the idea of loving your neighbor as yourself," or "following the golden rule," or "making the world a better place for everyone." In this way you frame the positive ethical actions of your children (with yourself as a model) in the context of spiritual ethics and values.

The Fifth Commandment—Family Harmony

This commandment teaches us that the family is the center and foundation of society.

It is a statement about the importance of family harmony and family members' responsibility to treat each other with respect, honor, and dignity. The Fifth Commandment reminds us that society only functions effectively when its children can experience emotional and spiritual stability and demonstrate respect for their parents and for those who created the world they have inherited.

The Fifth Commandment is not merely about showing respect for one's parents, it also refers to the profound level of commitment that each of us must have to creating order, purpose, and a reasonable degree of predictability in our society.

One of the most direct ways of reinforcing this important value in your children is by demonstrating your respect for *your* own parents. For example, when you do something like send a birthday or anniversary card to your parents, you can explain that your act is an expression of the Fifth Commandment to honor your father and mother. Your children can learn from you that taking care of you (the parent) is honoring the Fifth Commandment. Anytime your children are polite, thoughtful, or respectful of you, you can commend them for fulfilling this commandment with a positive spiritual act.

The Sixth Commandment—Don't Murder

The Sixth Commandment, "You shall not murder," is often mistranslated as "You shall not kill." Obviously murder is not the same as killing. In fact, the ancient Hebrew tradition (remember, the Ten Commandments were originally written in ancient Hebrew) specifically condones killing in self-defense, and teaches that if someone pursues you with the intent to kill, you are commanded to kill that person first.

In any event, when it comes to child raising, the Sixth Commandment is perhaps best understood as reflecting the fundamental religious value concerning the sanctity of life. Murder is morally wrong because all human life is sacred. Your job as a parent is to teach your child to value every human being as if that person carried a spark of the divine within.

The Sixth Commandment can be a challenge to raise your children to look for the good in other people. Murder and war ultimately come about because one human being is able to see another as not only less valuable, but somehow less human than he or she. That is why the "enemy" is always spoken of in negative, slang language designed to rob them of their humanity and distance them emotionally from us. "Kraut," "Jap," "Gook" are words that make human beings sound not human at all, and therefore make them easier to kill.

The Sixth Commandment can be used as a reminder that all people share the same hopes and dreams, frustrations, and desires no matter what their color, country of origin, or language. Teach your children not only to respect people who are different, but to see what can be learned from them as well. Stop them from using derogatory slang terms for other ethnic groups. Don't laugh at, tell, or permit others to tell derogatory ethnic jokes in your presence. In this way you teach the dignity of all people, the sanctity of all human life, and ultimately why the Sixth Commandment forbids us to murder another human being, no matter who he or she might be.

The Seventh Commandment—Don't Commit Adultery

"You shall not commit adultery," the Seventh Commandment, is naturally assumed to be a topic for adults only. The truth, however, is that what underlies this commandment is the importance of family stability, the importance that the Judeo–Christian tradition places on the institution of marriage, or creating committed loving relationships, and ultimately the importance of raising children who are able to commit to loving, nurturing, lasting relationships as well.

You prepare your children for this commandment when they are small, by teaching integrity, honesty, and trust. When you reward them for being honest (even if it's to tell you they did something they weren't supposed to), when you give praise each time you trust them and they come through for you, it builds the positive self-esteem so necessary for integrity and trustworthiness later in life.

The Seventh Commandment is necessary because we live in a world in which too many people are raised in families where there is precious little trust to begin with. Children need boundaries and a structure they can count on. They need mothers and fathers who give them unconditional love, who encourage them with praise and positive feedback, who build a world around them that is stable, secure, and safe. When this is done, they have a much better chance of being able to be trusted and relied upon when they grow up and are functioning in relationships as adults.

The Eighth Commandment—Don't Steal

Related to this need for developing positive self-esteem is the Eighth Commandment, "You shall not steal." Stealing for many is a reflection of an inner neediness that stems from a childhood filled with insecurity, tension, anxiety, and fear. Stealing is a negative way of exercising control over one's environment, by laying claim to things that otherwise are under the control of another.

The Eighth Commandment can serve as a teaching tool for emphasizing respect for others in an otherwise "me-first" world. You teach your children not to steal in different ways, depending upon their age level. For the younger child, a straightforward *quid pro quo* is all they can understand—you don't steal, because you don't want others to steal from you.

As kids get older, you can teach them that the primary reason for not stealing is because we are responsible for creating the kind of society in which we would like to live. We want to live in a world in which we can trust others, and others can trust us. We want to live in a world of integrity, fairness, justice, dignity, and compassion. To do so requires that we act in such a way as to bring the world closer to that model each day. "You shall not steal" is one of the rules necessary for such a world to exist both now and in the future.

The Ninth Commandment—Don't Lie

The Ninth Commandment is "You shall not bear false witness against your neighbor." It is directly related to the two preceding commandments, in that at its root its primary purpose is to reinforce the central importance of integrity in all relationships. The Ten Commandments are, in many ways, a blueprint for creating the ideal social order. They are guidelines that point to the key qualities and characteristics necessary for society to function at its best.

All social issues concern interpersonal relationships, whether between a person and his or her neighbor, loving partners, or parents and children. Contained within the simple, straightforward messages of the Ten Commandments are the fundamental principles necessary to establish order, security, trust, and human dignity.

"Bearing false witness" against another, in the language of children, is "lying." In fact, if you rephrase the Ninth

Commandment as "Don't lie," it is immediately clear how relevant this particular issue is to the lives of children.

Practically every child in the world lies at one time or another. It might be as relatively harmless as disclaiming responsibility for something they did, denying they broke one of the family behavior rules, claiming to have finished their homework when they haven't, or claiming that they didn't eat the last piece of cake in the refrigerator.

Lying for children is often a test of the adult world's tolerance and latitude toward unacceptable behavior. It is one of the ways that kids test for limits, search for boundaries, and ask (albeit unconsciously) for adult intervention. Part of your job as a parent, is to be clear about the importance of truth and honesty with your children, and to insist upon it at every opportunity.

Lying and the Loss of Faith

There are countless examples of the consequences that occur as a result of lying, particularly about other people. Lives and reputations have been ruined needlessly by unfounded slander, families and marriages torn apart by vicious rumors. Every child can provide personal recollections of occasions in their own lives when someone said something about them that wasn't true.

Ask them to recall such a time. How did they feel? How did they feel about the other person? What did they want to do about it? What could they do (if anything) to counteract what other people thought about them as a result of the untrue accusation? You might role play with your children an example of the damage that happens when gossip is spread about another person, and ask them to devise rules for behavior that might remind people how painful and harmful such experiences can be.

It undermines the very fabric of our society when people perjure themselves, and innocent people are found guilty of crimes they never committed. So, too, it destroys our ability to have faith in the people to whom we entrust the governing of our society when they take bribes and manipulate the legal and legislative system for personal gain, without regard to the impact on the lives of others. These are all instances in which someone has ignored the Ninth Commandment. Unfortunately, examples with which to teach our children are available practically every day in your local newspaper.

The Tenth Commandment—Appreciate What You Have

The Tenth Commandment reveals the single most important key to satisfaction in life. It is hidden in the commandment not to covet that which belongs to our neighbor. To "covet" something means to want something that isn't ours—to desire something that belongs to someone else. To properly understand the implications of this commandment is to discover what it takes to achieve fulfillment, satisfaction, and joy in life.

At its root, the Tenth Commandment really has nothing to do with other people at all. It revolves around the simple idea that one of the greatest sources of unhappiness in life is the feeling that we never have enough. The fact is, that no matter how much of anything we have, we could always have more—more money, more things, more friends, more houses, more cars, more vacation, more love.

Who Is Rich?

The wise sages of ancient Jewish life recognized that being happy has very little to do with how much money you make, the size of your home, or the toys that you accumulate. They ask the rhetorical question "Who is rich?" and reply "One who is happy with what he or she has." Frustration, anxiety, anger, jealousy, unhappiness are all a result of never being satisfied with our lot in life. Those who experience true joy in living are the ones who celebrate the blessings and gifts that they do have, rather than grumble over the things that they don't.

I believe the single best piece of advice that I have ever given my daughter Gable is to be happy about what she has rather than sad about what she doesn't have. The obsession that Americans have called "Keeping up with the Joneses" has probably sown more seeds of discontent than all the economic recessions and depressions in history.

Teaching your children to value and appreciate life as they live it, to have the ability to recognize the blessings and miracles that fill their lives each day, is one of the most important lessons you will ever pass on to them.

An easy way of getting across this lesson (and a good thing to do while riding in the car on a trip), is to sit down as a family and have everyone call out the things they have that they love the most. What are their favorite things in their rooms, at school, or at work? Who are their favorite friends and relatives? Where are their favorite places to go or things to see and do? How about the abilities, skills, and personality traits that they are most proud of?

After listing all these blessings that fill their lives, talk about all of the children in the world who have never had these opportunities, and probably will never experience the things your children are able to do. The idea isn't to feel guilty for what you have and others don't, it's to train yourself and your children to recognize the gifts and wonders that fill your lives each day.

The Tenth Commandment is a subtle program for fulfillment and happiness. Being able to appreciate whatever you have in life, whatever age you are, whatever stage of growth, learning, and development you are experiencing at the moment is the biggest key to satisfaction and happiness. Furthermore, the most wonderful part of it all is that this happiness is *totally* in your control, and the control of your children, for it depends on only one thing—their attitude.

The Power of Attitude

"Attitude" is probably the single most powerful word in the entire English language. Attitude is responsible for the very quality of your life and the lives of your children. It certainly isn't the specific experiences or circumstances of life that determine your happiness, it is rather the attitude that you bring to these experiences.

"You shall not covet" is a reminder that all happiness can come from within. Once basic needs for food, shelter, and love are met, the rest is determined by attitudes about life. Teaching your children to be happy with who they are, with what they have, with their own particular and unique talents and abilities, strengths, and weaknesses is giving them the gift of happiness in life.

Obviously there are hundreds of other ethical ideas, values, and lessons that you will want to share with your children. This chapter was designed to give you a start in the right direction, by sharing some of the major ethical ideas that form the foundation of what we call Judeo–Christian ethics. Now we move on to discover the ten most important keys to raising ethical children.

Five

Ten Keys to Raising Ethical Children

*The greatest natural resource that
any country can have is its children.*
                              Danny Kaye

While I was in the midst of writing this book, a remarkable story appeared on television news programs and in newspapers throughout Southern California. It was the true story of Tom and Pauline Nichter and their eleven-year-old son Jason, who had found a lost wallet containing $2,394 in cash, a credit card, a passport, and a plane ticket on the streets of Buena Park, California.

What made the story so remarkable was not only that they had turned all that money in to the police, who did manage to find its rightful owner (a visiting tourist from New Caledonia), but that Tom and Pauline were both jobless and homeless at the time! When even the police couldn't help but voice their amazement, Pauline simply replied, "All we did was what we were brought up to do—to be honest."

I watched her husband, Tom, being interviewed on the nightly news. His response to the questions of reporters, at what appeared to be such an outstanding act of honesty and integrity, was that yes, it was tempting to keep the money. But, he said, he kept thinking "What if this is all the money this person has in the world?" And Tom was painfully aware from his own recent life experiences how quickly one can go from living a normal life to being out on the streets, out of a job and homeless. He just couldn't keep the money.

What happened to them as a result of the news coverage was that people from all over the country reached into their own pockets and sent them contributions of every size. They both got offers for jobs, were helped to find an apartment in which to live with their son, and they ended up with over $16,000 from the generosity of strangers who were moved by their act of honesty and good citizenship.

As she gazed in shock at box after box of letters with donations that were sent to the Buena Park police station in their name, Pauline Nichter laughed and said, "This is all my mother's fault." And as I watched, I couldn't help but smile at the powerful lesson that eleven-year-old Jason had just learned about ethics from his mom and dad as well. He stood there in front of the cameras, beaming with pride at having done the right thing, and knowing first-hand that even in the worst of circumstances, he will always have the choice to follow his parents' outstanding model, in every decision that he makes.

"This is all my mother's fault." Wouldn't that be music to our ears if we were Pauline Nichter's mother? To realize what a profound ethical effect we had on our child through the moral lessons that we taught and the examples that we set. This has always been and always will be the single most important key to raising ethical children—BE A MORAL MODEL PERIOD!

1. Be a Moral Model

Moral modeling is key number one, for it transcends every other kind of lesson that we might hope to teach. "Do as I say, not as I do" is a fanciful wish that just doesn't ever hold water when it comes to ethical behavior. Our children learn from watching, not from listening to our preaching (and as a rabbi, I should know!). I believe it was the poet Wordsworth who once wrote, "I cannot hear your words, for what you are is thundering in my ears." That is a reality of parenting that simply cannot be avoided, skirted, evaded, or ignored. What you are, how you act, what you do—*these* are the truly important lessons that you teach day in and day out to your children.

That isn't to say that words are unimportant—they aren't. What you say does make a difference, it's just that the impact is so miniscule compared to the sledgehammer impact that your actions make on your children. The real value of words, of lectures, or moral lessons and ethical sayings that you can teach to your children, is to *reinforce* your behavior with an intellectual, philosophical, and spiritual framework that sets your behavior in a larger social context.

The verbal lessons that you teach your children about how to behave ethically in the world, are important to the degree that they compliment and are consistent with the actual ways that they see you behave in your daily life. Unfortunately, when it comes to raising your children, you just can't get away with very much. They know when your words and actions don't add up. They know when you don't "practice what you preach," and when that happens you are teaching them that when it comes to the realm of ethics, they should expect the world to be hypocritical. After all, if that is how they experience their own parents, the ultimate source of ethics and morality in their universe, why should they ever expect anything else from the rest of the world?

Ethics by Illustration

Without question, the old cliché that "Children learn what they live" continues to be the single most important lesson for parents to learn about raising ethical children. Over the years I have worked with parents and teachers of all ages and backgrounds in workshops on values, ethics, and discipline in both the home and school. I have often asked them to relate examples of how their own parents influenced their values.

I am sure that it will come as no surprise for you to learn, that one hundred percent of the time, the most important way that adults felt their own parents passed on values to them, was simply by example. One hundred percent of the time ethical adults, parents, and teachers could recount examples from the behavior of their own parents that illustrated the values they were trying to impart.

This learning was ethics by illustration, role modeling of the very best sort, usually informally, simply through watching how their parents actually lived their lives, interacted with others, talked about their friends, neighbors, co-workers, children, and the like. The truth is that these have always been the single most powerful lessons that any of us have learned.

Take a moment while you are reading this to think about your own parents and teachers. Recall any significant moments of your life in which you learned an important ethical lesson from your parents or another significant adult role model. I guarantee that it was most effectively taught to you through example, and not solely through word of mouth.

Pithy, easy to remember ethical sayings can be helpful, but they are never enough. Christians often quote the sayings of Jesus in the New Testament, and Jews used to begin every morning worship service with a reading of the "Saying of the Ancestors," a collection of ethical and moral aphorisms from the sages of Jewish tradition, so that they would begin the day being reminded of the ideal behavior they were expected to emulate.

Even so, these catchy moral sayings are simply verbal reminders of the behavior that we are supposed to have experienced through the everyday ethical acts of the significant adults in our lives, primarily our parents and teachers. If the ethical role models are absent, all the

powerful sayings in the world will not create ethical children.

Doing the Right Thing

One quick example from my own family occurred a couple
of years ago, when my wife and daughter were getting out
of their car in a shopping mall. When my daughter, Gable,
opened the car door, it accidently banged into the next car
and made a small white mark on the other car.

My wife immediately went to get a pad and paper and
started writing a note. Gable asked her, "What are you
doing?" and she replied, "I'm leaving a note for the owner
of the other car so he or she can get in touch with me."
Gable then said, "But why don't we just leave? No one is
around so no one would know about it."

Didi answered, "What do you mean no one would
know? The two most important people will always know—
you and I. Always remember the saying 'What goes around
comes around.' Although it may not come back in exactly
the same way, when you put out good into the world, it
comes back to you one way or another, and when you put
out bad into the world, it comes back as well. This is simply
the right thing to do."

The truth is that at the time Gable still really didn't
understand why they didn't just go into the shopping center
quickly so no one would see, and simply "get away with it,"
since that was the stage of her own developmental thinking.

What was really amazing was when shopping in another
center just one month later, Gable and Didi came out only
to find a note on *their* car from a stranger who had done
exactly the same thing to my wife's car. Gable immediately
exclaimed, "Look mommy, you were right! It came back to
us already."

Now I can't promise that even reading this book will guarantee that you will always have such a one-to-one direct payback for the ethical acts that you perform in life, but what is important is to recognize the teachable moments when they arise and jump on them. One way or another, the opportunity to point out that "good deeds" also get done to those who do them to others will present itself if you are always open to seeing the acts of goodness that surround us each day.

2. Use the Power of Positive Reinforcement

When professional educators want to communicate to parents the importance of encouraging their children to behave in ways that their parents approve of, they usually will be heard endorsing what is commonly called "positive reinforcement." Positive reinforcement simply teaches us that if we want someone to act in a certain way, we will have the best results if we reward that person for the behavior that we desire.

Everyone practices one form or another of positive reinforcement throughout their lives, whether they recognize it as such or not. For example, babies quickly learn, long before they can even talk or conceptualize what they are doing, that if they cry in a certain way, for a certain length of time, they can train their mother (or father) to either (A) bend down and pick them up, (B) feed them, or (C) change their uncomfortable dirty diaper.

This is probably the first form of positive reinforcement that we experience, since after the parent has complied with the desired behavior, the baby inevitably *stops crying*, thereby giving the parent exactly the reward that was desired. This rather crude (but effective) form of early positive reinforcement training simply continues in one form or another throughout our lives.

We experience it with parents and teachers, and they experience it in turn with us. When young people first begin to date, they quickly master the appropriate cues both verbal and physical that give just enough positive reinforcement to their date to encourage or discourage them from behaving as they wish them to behave.

All of us have this ability, and to one degree or another we all practice forms of positive reinforcement with the significant people in our lives. We all know the basic rule, that to achieve the desired behavioral results from those around us, we need to apply the appropriate amount of positive reinforcement for the given situation at hand.

When it comes to raising ethical children, the same rule regarding the importance of positive reinforcement applies. The only difference is that here we are trying to inculcate within the fabric of our children's lives an almost automatic ethical response to whatever real-life situation might arise. Our dream is to grow up to discover that we are Pauline Nichter's mother, having raised a child to whom honesty, justice, and compassion are second nature.

The second key to raising ethical children is to get yourself into the frame of mind where instead of looking out for things that your children do wrong—acting like a watchdog constantly waiting for them to transgress one of your parental "commandments" so that you can pounce—you surprise them with exactly the opposite.

Positively Impacting Children's Self-Worth

Imagine the impact on your children's sense of self-worth and esteem if you were constantly on the lookout to *catch them doing something right.* What's more, imagine how differently your own perceptions of your children would be, if instead of noticing what they do wrong all the time, you spent your energy searching for the things they do well, the characteristics they exhibit of which you are proud, the acts of kindness, caring, and sensitivity which reflect the true quality of their character.

This is a wonderful, inspiring, and truly empowering approach to raising your children, which is borrowed from the successful strategies that have helped make American corporations so outstanding in the area of personal motivation. Just as it works well in the corporate world, so too it can work wonders at home with your children. I often have heard it said by the wisest of educators, that ultimately everyone in life just needs a little attention. That is particularly so with children—they will get attention just about any way they can. If they can't get it in a positive way, they will still crave attention so much that they will get it in a negative way.

The key here is that once you realize how important attention is to a child, you will reward that child with *positive* attention for the behaviors that you desire, realizing that this is the single best way to reinforce in that child's inner psyche the importance of experiencing that behavior as an integral part of his or her being and self image.

When you think of the phrase "Catch them doing something right," let it remind you from time to time that your children are already acting in caring, sensitive, appropriate ways, but your tendency (if you are like most) is to ignore them unless they act out negatively. The challenge is to catch them acting in the positive ways that you approve of, and then be sure to give them as many rewards, and as much reinforcement and support as you can. In this way, when they need attention they will be more likely to seek it by acting in a way that will make you proud so that you will reward their behavior with your approval.

3. Listen with Your Eyes

One of the primary ways we express our love for another is through the simple act of listening to them when they talk to us. When someone listens to what we have to say, it inevitably makes us feel valuable, worthwhile, important to that person. Most of us have had both positive and negative experiences with this notion. For example, you may recall standing up in front of a class and giving a report or a speech, or sharing "What I did this summer," only to discover that the kids in the class weren't paying much attention. I remember being devastated by this experience as a small child (and I *was* very small as a child), so that I resolved never to have that happen again.

From then on I was pretty much the class clown, often drawing attention to myself in negative ways just to ensure that I wasn't ignored. Having the attention of those around me, whether students or teachers even if it was for negative reasons, at least let me know that I existed to them, that who I was had an impact and made a difference one way or another.

The same is true with the people you love. Whether they are your spouse, parent, loving companion, or child, knowing that you will pay attention to them when they speak and listen to what they have to say sends them the undeniable message that they are important in your eyes.

I have the rather unfortunate ability to do several things at the same time without being confused. I can often be reading one thing and carrying on a conversation with someone at the same time. As a result, I can't even count the number of times that I have been startled in the midst of a conversation with either Didi (my wife) or Gable (my daughter) by one of them rather crossly and impatiently saying, "You're not paying attention to what I'm saying," even though I know that I am.

Each time I realize once again that because I'm not *watching* them as they are speaking, I am giving them the message that they are less important to me at that moment than whatever else it is I am doing. The hard truth is that *listening* to others is one of the most important and direct ways that we communicate our love to them. The simple act of looking at them while they speak, giving them our full attention, communicates more directly than almost anything else we do, that we truly think they are worthy of that attention. What this insight teaches us is that we have at our disposal each day a simple, yet powerful way that we can help to nurture a feeling of positive self-esteem in our children. What we need to do, is to give them two of our most valuable possessions, our time and attention. It is clearly one of the most powerful ways we have of giving those we love the message of how important they are to us.

Children Want to Be Heard

It reminds me of the story of the child who came home from school to find his father busying himself in the kitchen making dinner. The child began to relate the story of his adventures at school that day and without looking up from his work, from time to time the father would grunt "uhh huh...." After a couple of minutes the little boy said to his father with a note of irritation in his voice, "You aren't listening to me!"

The father glanced up for a moment from the stove and responded, "Of course I'm listening to you." "But daddy," the little boy replied, "You're not listening with your *eyes*."

That's our challenge, too. Listening with our eyes. Whether or not we like it, there is just no substitute for the validation and acknowledgment that our children receive from the simple act of watching them as they speak to us. Listening with your eyes tells them that they are special, that they are valuable, that there is nothing you would rather do and no place you would rather be than right there listening to them.

Listening with your eyes is really a marvelous gift of the heart, and one which you can give to your children every day. It is a gift that costs nothing, yet makes the recipient feel like a million dollars. I realize that this seems like simple, perhaps even simplistic advice. With all the sophisticated research that has taken place in the fields of child development, educational theory, and the like in every university in the world for decades, here I am suggesting that one of the most important parenting rules to remember is, "listen with your eyes." I know how it may sound, yet I can't stress it enough. Give your children the gift of your attention, your eyes firmly fixed on them and nothing else, and they will truly feel worthwhile, valued, and loved.

Children want to be heard, and they want to feel that they are being understood. They want to feel that what they have to say counts for something, that their opinions are valued especially by adults. When you think about it, all of us have the same needs and desires. No matter how old we are, one of the key ways that we judge our own importance in the eyes of others is the degree to which what we have to say seems to be important to them. That is why listening is one of the most important gifts you can give your children. And it's free!

4. Be Consistent

Children need stability and consistency in their lives. One of the most difficult challenges that caring parents have to face when it comes to effective discipline and the desire to raise ethical children is the need to be consistent in how they react to the behavior of their children.

This doesn't mean that you are expected to react exactly the same way each and every time your child forgets to make his bed or brush her teeth before going to bed. What it does mean is that children need to live in a world that they can count on. They need the external security of knowing what to expect from their environment, so that they can successfully develop the internal security that they need to succeed in life as adults.

Next to being fed, clothed, and housed, and almost as important as feeling loved and valued by their parents, the most important need that children have is for security and stability. Environmental stability encourages emotional stability in children, as they often subconsciously take their cues regarding how safe and secure they are emotionally from how safe and secure they seem to be physically.

Encouraging an Attitude of Openness

One of the goals of successful parenting is to encourage your children to experiment with the world around them. You want your children to be open to new experiences, to have the internal strength to venture out to new places, to be able to easily develop new relationships with other children, and to approach the world with a sense of eagerness and curiosity. You want your children to develop the expectation that rather than the world being a hostile and capricious place, it is filled with wonderful and exciting opportunities for learning, growth, and discovery.

Believe it or not, one of the most important ways that you can help your children to develop an attitude of openness toward the world around them is by raising them in an environment that communicates stability, security, and consistency. Being consistent with your responses to their behavior both good and bad teaches them in the most direct, concrete way possible that there are things about their world that are dependable and can be counted upon.

Few things create greater insecurity for your children than never being kissed or hugged or told that they are loved and competent, or never knowing how their parents are going to react to anything that they do. When children misbehave and their parents react one time by making them sit in the corner of their room for twenty minutes by themselves, and the next time by simply ignoring it, the children never get a clear message about the inappropriateness of the behavior.

Tempering Consistency with Reason

The goal is to be as consistent as you can, within reason. Ralph Waldo Emerson once said, "A foolish consistency is the hobgoblin of little minds . . . ," and he was right. "Being consistent" for its own sake, with little regard for the nature, quality, and impact of the responses that you have chosen to be consistent about, may very well be a "foolish consistency" after all. Everything that you do must be tempered with reason and balance. Sometimes there may be mitigating circumstances, other problems that have arisen within the family or with a particular child, that will cause you to decide not to react in the predictable fashion.

As long as you are making conscious choices regarding your parenting decisions and the messages that you are sending to your children, you will most likely be just fine. We probably do the most damage, and undermine the ethical parenting that we are striving to accomplish, when we act and react with very little or no real thought regarding the impact that our various decisions are having on the emotional lives of our children.

Our children's fate is truly in our hands every day. Not only are they dependent on us for their physical well-being and sustenance, but they also rely upon our feedback for their emotional well-being. Being consistent in your reactions to the behavior of your children, both in what you praise and what you punish, is a key to nurturing their own ability to develop an internal behavior regulator.

The Internal Parent

Ultimately your goal is have your voice be heard in the minds of your children, even when you aren't around. Each of has had this experience ourselves, at one time or another. Each of us has been about to do something that we knew we shouldn't do, only to "hear" the voice of our mother or father, a teacher or coach, older brother, sister, or grandparent—whoever served as one of our primary ethical role models and teachers—telling us that they disapproved. If you are like most people, hearing that "internal parent" voice probably changed the way you actually behaved.

One of the goals of ethical parenting is to create just such a voice in the minds of our children. This isn't as insidious or devious as it may at first blush appear, since all of us have lots of voices that echo within our minds from the vast reservoir of experiences that we have encountered during the course of our lives. All I am pointing out is that when it comes to ethical behavior, and the sometimes difficult ethical choices that your children will have to make in their lives, it is preferable that the internal voice they listen to be yours—not the disc jockey on the radio, the video jockey on MTV, or the kids in the school yard.

5. Have Integrity, Mean What You Say

Without establishing yourself as a model of trust and integrity for your children, it becomes much more difficult to successfully raise your children to be ethical, morally sensitive human beings. Parents simply *must* be trustworthy. Your word must stand for something. If you tell your children that you will take them to Disneyland, and then never do, you lose credibility. If you make promises out of frustration, just so that you can cope with their demands of the moment, without ever truly planning on fulfilling those promises, you are teaching your children to lie. Not only are you modeling behavior that you really don't want them to emulate, but by demonstrating that they can't really trust your word or count on you to mean what you say regarding inconsequential matters, you end up undermining your credibility in more serious matters as well.

There is an old airline saying that a passenger who sees that the ashtrays are dirty will assume that the engine is in equally ill repair. All of us generalize from the particular. That's just the way the human mind seems to work. We take our own narrow, limited-focus experiences, and we assume that the rest of the world is simply a larger reflection of those same personal experiences.

So too with our children. They may not recall the exact promises broken (although if yours are like mine, they probably will), but you can be sure that they will know that your word really can't be counted on. What I am describing here is fundamentally a very simple concept—when you say something to your children, make sure that you mean it. The underlying reason is that you not only want your children to trust you and listen to you when you speak, you also want them to be trustworthy themselves. We all want our children to grow up to be the kind of people whom others can rely on, whose word is gold, who have reputations for being reliable, trustworthy individuals with integrity. Integrity is something they learn from you—like most things, not by what you preach, but by how you live your life each day.

Integrity and trust come in many forms, but all of them have to do with keeping your commitments, whatever they may be. When your children grow up knowing that if you tell them you will be home from an evening out at 10:30 P.M. and they wake up at 11:00 P.M. you will be there, it is much easier for them to understand why you might expect the same in return when they begin to go out as teenagers.

Setting curfews and expecting your children to honor them are simple examples of a general principle of great importance. I can't emphasize enough, that what you do and how you act are truly of major significance to your children. They either learn that keeping one's word is important, or they learn that what someone says doesn't really have to be taken all that seriously. If that is the lesson they absorb, then they will have great difficulty developing the attitude that keeping their commitments is an important reflection of their honesty and integrity as people.

Learning Integrity

Every day that you spend with your children brings more opportunities to teach lessons in integrity and trust. You can begin when they are young by giving them small, easily managed tasks to complete, like carrying silverware to help set the table for dinner, putting away laundry or cleaning up in the bathroom, and then let the chores get increasingly complex as they grow older each year. The connection between doing chores around the house and learning integrity and trust, lies in the context within which you assign the tasks.

For example, if every time your children complete a job that you have given them to do, you tell them how proud you are that you can trust them to keep their word and follow through on whatever commitments they make, it creates a link in their minds between keeping their word, and earning the respect and admiration of the people they love most.

Everything teaches something. Every time you react positively to some way in which your children have demonstrated that they can be trusted, you are teaching them how important the quality of trust is to you. One of the best chances that we have for our children to grow up to be caring, ethical adults is if we train them as children to feel proud of themselves when they demonstrate that they can be counted on to keep their word.

I believe in the importance of integrity above all. Integrity forms a strong ethical foundation upon which all other ethical action can be based. Principle, honor, decency, honesty, and character all flow from the bedrock of integrity. In one sense, our integrity is one of those rare commodities that no one can take away from us. However, since young children can't conceptualize such things on their own, we must find appropriate ways to teach them what integrity is all about.

Teaching Using Children's Heroes

Perhaps one way, aside from role modeling (which is always the most important way), is to use the heroes that attract our children's attention and admiration. After all, integrity is one of the main ingredients of which these heroes are made. Perhaps a good way to begin instilling integrity in our children is to bring attention to those moments in the movies and on television programs, where the hero performs an act that is a natural expression of his or her integrity, or acts in a way that you would want your children to emulate. Even a simple "Isn't it nice that Steven Seagal always goes to help those in need," or "I liked that in *Forever Young* Mel Gibson fixed the roof and the plumbing of the house of that family that was kind to him," will do some good.

The Still, Small Voice of Conscience

Another good technique is to point out to your children when someone (including themselves) resists a temptation for the sake of maintaining their own integrity. It might be returning someone's wallet, giving back money given to you incorrectly for change, behaving yourself in spite of the fact that there is no one to see you misbehave, or doing the right thing even when the wrong thing might feel better to you at that moment in time. The question that you want to have your children ask themselves almost automatically throughout their lives is "When this moment is over and I'm looking back at myself from a future point in time, will I be proud of the person that I'm remembering?"

If you can instill this kind of reflexive self-examination in your children at an early age, it will stay with them throughout their lives. Then they will carry the still, small voice of conscience within, and it will remind them each day that one of the most precious and irreplaceable gifts they will ever have is the gift of their own integrity.

6. Demonstrate Unconditional Love

Raising ethical children begins above all else with unconditional love. Showing your child acceptance and love from his or her first year of life is the foundation of all ethical action. Our prisons are filled with adults who as children were rejected, unloved, and emotionally abused by their parents. Whether Charles Manson or Robert Alton Harris, psychopathic killers inevitably share the same tragic beginnings—they were often unloved by their parents, uncared for, rejected, shunted aside, and abused.

Positive loving attachment to a parent figure is the first crucial step toward building the requisite self-esteem and self-image necessary for ethical social behavior as an adult. Holding, touching, kissing, demonstrating love for your children from their earliest infancy is the single most important gift you can give them. It is the one linchpin that holds all the other emotional, social, psychological, and spiritual building blocks of personality together. Without it, your children are doomed to a life of inner conflict, pain, and turmoil. With it, anything is possible and there are no limits to what they can accomplish. Nothing can hold them back from becoming the kind of people that any of us would be proud to have in our lives.

The great American philosopher, writer, and teacher William James once wrote that "The deepest principle of human beings is the craving to be appreciated." These simple words reflect, indeed, the deepest cry of the human heart for love. James rightly recognized that within every human breast beats a heart crying out for at least one other human being to reach back in return. As we will learn in Chapter 6, it is upon feeling that we are loved and lovable that all fundamental feelings of self-worth are ultimately based.

A Gift Only You Can Give

For our children to grow up able to extend their own hands to others, they need the security of feeling deep within their souls that they are valuable, capable, competent, and lovable. Only parents have the power to bestow this precious gift upon their children. It is a spiritual inheritance within the grasp of everyone, regardless of race, religious, language, profession, or financial solvency. Giving your children the blessing of unconditional love is, without question, the single most important gift you will ever give.

"Unconditional love" does not mean that you don't discipline your children, correct them when they are wrong, or punish them when they misbehave. It often isn't what you do, it's how you do it. Even strict rules clearly enforced within a home can communicate unconditional love to children, if their parents consistently demonstrate with affection, touching, hugging, and kissing, along with verbal praise and encouragement that the love they have for their children is not dependent upon specific behavior from moment to moment.

The real test of unconditional love lies in the word "unconditional." It means that our love for our children doesn't come and go each day, dependent upon whether or not they happened to obey our commands, do their homework on time, clean up their rooms, take out the trash, leave a sweater at school, or get into a fight with a friend.

Unconditional means just that—without conditions. It means we love them for who they are, not for how they act from moment to moment. In fact it means that they are worthy of our love simply because they are our children, and not merely because they are "good" children, or "obedient" children, or "quiet" children.

Unconditional love is crucial to the emotional health of every child. It is necessary for them to feel valuable enough to extend that same love to others when the time comes, thereby bringing more compassion and love into the world instead of less.

Separate Behavior from the Child

Demonstrating such love for our children is not always easy. With all the times that we are irritated or upset by our kids, it is often very hard to separate the child from the behavior. It's so easy for us to inappropriately lash out with our parental judgment reflex at our children, even yelling in the upset of the moment that they are bad, stupid, rotten, wicked, dumb, irresponsible, thoughtless, undependable, or untrustworthy.

What would get across the point that we are upset and disapprove of what our children have done, yet keep intact the unconditional nature of our love for them at the same time, is to concentrate on the behavior and not on the child. It may seem like a small thing, perhaps too subtle to mean anything at all, but it truly makes a big difference to our children whether or not they hear us condemning their *behavior,* or condemning *them.*

It isn't who they are that we are upset about, it is what they have done. They may have done something irresponsible or thoughtless, but they and their behavior are not identical. It's much better for their emotional well-being and ultimate sense of self-worth to hear us chastising their behavior than castigating the essential nature of their being. After all, we do love them, even when we hate something that they have done. What we want to avoid at all costs is our children getting the message that rather than their behavior, it is actually them that we hate.

Demonstrate Love Daily

The key is to keep in mind at all times the importance not only of knowing that you want to give your children unconditional love, but of *demonstrating* that unconditional love each day. Some people find it a good technique to actually practice finding two ways each day to demonstrate their love for their children. These aren't supposed to be physical ways, like bringing home a present every day, but emotional gifts, like hugging, kissing, positive reinforcement for who they are, verbal acknowledgment of your love and their inherent value, and the like. In this way, parents, too, become habituated to relating to their children from a position of unconditional love, and children get the constant emotional nourishment and support that they so deeply need.

7. When They Ask "Why?" Tell Them

One of the most frustrating experiences in a child's life is to ask his or her parents why they think it's important to act in a certain way, only to hear the infamous universal parental reply, "Because I said so, that's why!" All you need to do is think back to your own childhood and I'm sure you will easily remember how truly exasperating such an answer was at the time.

When kids ask you why it's important to *you* that they act in a particular way, I believe that most of the time they do really want to know. It isn't always just a verbal stalling technique to avoid acting, which is how most parents treat such a question. Rather, it is the child "as student" asking the parents "as teachers" exactly what makes such behavior important or desirable to them.

If you treat all questions by your children as serious and important, you will discover that there are many positive repercussions. First, it lets them know that who they are and what they have to say is important to you. Second, it tells them that they are important enough for you to take the time to answer their question and not simply ignore or dismiss them as a nuisance. Third, it trains them to ask questions that they really do want the answers to, since if you routinely take all their questions seriously, they quickly learn that if they don't want to know something, they better not ask in the first place. Once they have internalized that you are conscientious about your role as parent–teacher, you, too, will know that the questions they ask are truly of interest to them.

Tell Them What You Believe

Now I am not suggesting that your job is to be a stand-up encyclopedia at all times; rather it is to be open, honest, and direct with your children about why you believe that certain behavior is important to do and other behavior is important not to do. It's not an issue of needing to be the answer person for every question, but of speaking the truth about issues of ethics, morality, and social behavior.

I'm reminded of the story of the child who asked his father one day, "Daddy, why did the apple turn brown after you cut it open?" The father then replied, "Well, son, you see the acid in the apples interacts with the oxygen in the air in such a way as to produce a condition called oxidation, which then turns the color of the apples from white to brown." At this point the boy looked up at his father and said, "Daddy, are you talking to me?"

It isn't the scientific explanation of oxidation that our children are hungering for, it is the knowledge of right and wrong, an understanding of what values are important to you their parents, and why you feel strongly about the ideals and ethical goals to which you are committed.

Your children deserve to know that you believe strongly enough in your own set of ethical and moral rules not only to live them out in your own life through your own actions, but to be able to tell them why these values are important to you as well. It can be as simple as, "If you treat other people the way you would like to be treated, then you will

always be making the world a better place in which to live."
Or perhaps, "It's important to treat all people with respect,
because then you become an example for others to follow.
The more that people act like you, the better the world will
be for everyone."

Even simple explanations such as these will give your
children a firm grounding in the rationale for your values.
Naturally, religious people tend to ground their values in
their understanding of what God wants them to do. Their
response to a child's question regarding why act in a certain way might simply be, "Because I believe that is what
God wants us to do," or perhaps "Because 'Don't steal' is
written in the Ten Commandments (or the Bible)."

Whatever explanation is true for you is the explanation
that you ought to give to your children. Don't make up reasons just to have an answer. Think about why these values
that you are teaching to your children are important to
you, and then share those reasons, whatever they may actually be, with your children. In that way your ethical value
system will be greatly strengthened, you will have a much
more secure understanding of the reasons for both your
own behavior and the social and ethical rules that you are
teaching your children, and you will be giving an important spiritual gift to your entire family.

8. Give Them What They Need, Not What They Want

Every parent knows that just because their children ask for
something, isn't a good enough reason to give it to them.
To use a silly example, if your children asked you for ice
cream, candy, and popcorn for dinner every night, you certainly wouldn't give it them, even though that's what they

were asking for. The same must be true for issues of behavior, ethics, and values.

Just because your children ask you to let them stay out at night until two o'clock in the morning with their friends, or get a tattoo, or see an R- or even X-rated movie, isn't a good enough reason to let them. Your role is always to be the parent and teacher, guide and mentor, not merely their companion or friend. Your children aren't your peers, they are your responsibility. What is important, is that at all times, even when it seems the farthest possible thing from their minds, they are looking to you for limits and guidance against which to measure their own behavior.

This is true when your children are young, and it remains true (just a lot harder to recognize) as they grow older. Even in the midst of their most rebellious teen years, children want to know that their parents have values that are solid, that can be counted on, and that will give them moral moorings in an otherwise seemingly value-free and frightening world. That is your role, today, tomorrow, and always. Give them what they need, not the emotional, physical, and spiritual junk food that they think they want, and they will be grateful to you in the long run.

9. Give Them a Sense of Belonging

One of the least recognized needs that children have is the simple need to belong. Too often our tendency is to think of ethical behavior in personal, individual terms, and not as a set of rules and expectations that occur within the greater context of belonging to a group or community. When we teach our children the right way to act to be the kind of people that we want them to grow up to become, it is always because the fundamental reality of life is that we live it within community, among other striving, searching, and growing human beings like ourselves.

As a result of how we human beings are created, we have this innate need to be connected to other human beings, to feel our relationship with them, to experience ourselves as a part of something larger than just our mere individual lives. This is a gift that you can give to your children—the gift of belonging.

Every child needs to feel that he or she is not alone in the world. This need to belong is part of the fundamental human desire for transcending our aloneness, and for feeling that we are cared for and loved by someone else. To grow up emotionally whole and spiritually secure, children need first and foremost to feel the love of their parents and family. They need to know deep within that they are not alone, that there are others, or at least one other in this world who truly loves them, cares about them, watches out for them, and takes care of them.

Feeling Connected

Out of the basic human need for feeling loved and cared for grows the equally important need for feeling connected to other human beings. This is the need to belong. That is why people join organizations, feel such fierce loyalty to their alma maters, athletic teams, social clubs, or even religious institutions. You can help meet those important needs in your own children in many ways, such as by joining churches, mosques, or synagogues in your community; encouraging them to participate in 4-H Clubs, service clubs at school, or other team activities.

Feeling connected to others is an important prerequisite for feeling responsible for the welfare of others. The most dangerous people in our society are the sociopaths who feel no connection whatsoever to other human beings, and who therefore have no difficulty causing others pain, suffering, and even death.

Raising ethical children requires that you create opportunities for your children to feel this connection with others as strongly as possible. It requires you to be constantly aware of the importance of nurturing within them a feeling of belonging to the larger community within which they must always live. For ethical children to become ethical adults, they must experience their own lives as integrally a part of the lives of others. Only then will they feel the deeply rooted sense of social responsibility that is your goal.

10. Respect Them and Demand Respect in Return

In many ways, the core of moral social behavior is respect. It is at the heart of the Golden Rule, to do unto others as you would have them do unto you. Treating kids with respect, creating an ethical environment for them in which to grow up and experience family life, means to treat them as valuable human beings with their own inner worth, self-respect, and dignity.

Dr. Bruno Bettelheim taught that if we don't base our parenting on respect for our children, they will not take morality and ethics seriously, for it will always appear to be a sham, manufactured in the abstract primarily for the purposes of impressing others. If they don't feel that they are worthy enough as human beings to warrant the respect of their parents, then it becomes impossible for them to internalize the need to demonstrate that same respect for others.

Raising ethical children involves establishing an environment within your home that nurtures through actual living on a practical level the same values that you desire to impart to your children on a theoretical level. For example, to encourage your children to show respect for the opinions of others, you must demonstrate in your daily interactions with them that you actually respect their opinions as well.

This is true at every age, but particularly true when it comes to teenagers. You must learn to strike a balance between asserting your own authority and decisions when you feel they are warranted, and demonstrating your respect for your children by allowing them the freedom to make choices for themselves as well.

Parenting, Not a Popularity Contest

It is important to remember that parenting isn't a popularity contest. Your goal isn't to become your child's best friend, it is to give them the love and moral inspiration that will help them to grow up to be caring and intelligent young adults.

That is why I constantly remind parents that part of the responsibility of parenting is to make the unpopular and sometimes uncomfortable decisions that allow you to the best of your ability to keep your children safe, protecting them from themselves or from getting into situations where they are asking for trouble.

If you make a decision and your children continue to protest strongly or insist that you are being unreasonable and treating them like young children, it is usually worth taking the time to hear them out calmly and rationally. Sit down with them and let them try to persuade you that another choice would be just as good or better. Let them do their best to convince you that together you can work out a compromise or a joint solution that will make everyone happy while respecting both your standards of behavior and their expectations of themselves.

When you can approach each parenting decision with your children knowing that not only do you love them, but you respect them as individuals with their own inner dreams and goals, their own needs and desires, then you will have established the kind of relationship that encourages them to constantly rise to the best that lies within each of them.

These then are ten of the keys necessary to unlock the door to raising ethical children. Along with a knowledge of moral development, an understanding of what is appropriate behavior to expect from your children at any given age and a clearly articulated set of behavioral expectations and consequences, you will be well on the road to raising the kind of children who will help make the world a much more caring and ethical place in which we all can live.

Six

The Power of Positive Self-Esteem

There is no value judgment more important to man—no factor more decisive in his psychological development and motivation—than the estimate he passes on himself.

Nathaniel Brandon

Imagine that you had it in your power t
one gift above all others. If you coulc
the one possession, quality, or characteristic u.
your estimation help them the most to create lives of su
cess, purpose, meaning, satisfaction, and joy, what would
that one gift be? Wealth? Fame? Intelligence? Physical
beauty? Charm? Strength? When all is said and done, the
single most important gift that you could ever give to your
children would be *the gift of positive self-esteem.*

In his book *Raising Good Children* Thomas Lickona
describes the results of studies done at the University of
California by Dr. Stanley Coopersmith of various kids who
demonstrated either high or low self-esteem. In his study,
he discovered that there were clearly identifiable differences in the family backgrounds of these children, and
reinforced the important role that parental behavior and
role modeling play in creating successful self-images
among children.

In this study, Dr. Coopersmith discovered that parents
of high self-esteem kids generally demonstrated more love
and acceptance of their children through simple everyday
expressions of affection and attention than did the parents
of kids with low self-esteem. The parents of low self-esteem
kids tended, on the other hand, to be highly critical and
vocally judgmental of their children all the time.

At the same time, contrary to what popular culture and
wisdom might suggest, the parents of high self-esteem children were less permissive and more consistent when it
came to setting clear, unambiguous, and realistic expectations of their children's behavior, with rules that everyone
understood. Children with low self-esteem generally had
parents who were inconsistent, and unclear about their
expectations, and either never set rules at all or just didn't
follow through on rules once they were set.

Perhaps it is simply the result of absorbing the culture and values of living in the open, democratic societies of North America, but whatever the reason might be, children with high self-esteem tended to come from families with an overall democratic tone and practice. Such children grew up believing that their opinions mattered, even at a young age. Throughout their lives they knew from first-hand experience that their parents paid attention to them and to their needs and wants, and took their suggestions and contributions seriously.

When there are consistent, appropriate demonstrations of acceptance, attention, and approval that children receive from their parents, these acts are inevitably translated in their children's minds as signifying "I am worthwhile, valuable, and lovable." And above all others, there is perhaps no greater lesson that our children can learn than that they are fundamentally valuable, worthwhile human beings. The belief in themselves that this knowledge engenders empowers our children with the inner security necessary to give respect and love to others in return.

I believe that parenting is the task of leading our children on a unique treasure hunt, where they are the treasure. It is an adventure in self-discovery that requires parents to serve as guides, cheerleaders, sources of inspiration, and models of ideal behavior. One of the most important tasks we have as we lead our children on this "treasure hunt for the self," is to empower them to see themselves as having the capability and competence to be successful in this life-long challenging task of self-discovery.

Celebrating Their Uniqueness

The task of helping our children realize that they are essentially good human beings is truly monumental. One of the primary tools at our disposal in this great educational challenge is the realization of the miracle of their uniqueness. We must help them to understand that not only is their very existence a miracle, but even more remarkable and miraculous is the fact that even though there are some five billion human beings alive on this planet, *no two are exactly alike*. That means that there is only one them in all the world. No one, no matter how smart, how beautiful, how strong, how clever, how talented, how brilliant, or how rich, can *ever* be a better version of them than they can. They will always be the best at being themselves, and their true challenge in life is simply to make that unique self the very best it can be.

The reason that this is such an important self-esteem tool is that throughout our lives it seems as if who we are is under constant scrutiny by nearly everyone we meet. From parents and teachers, siblings and peers, co-workers and bosses, boy and girl friends, and spouses, we too often feel that there is some external, objective, almost mythical universal standard of behavior, competence, social skills, and physical attraction against which we are being compared. Such a constant sense of comparison to the ideal can only lead most of us to feel in some ways inferior, less than adequate to the task of successfully negotiating the challenges that life has to offer.

With children this sense of always being in the center of a universal judgmental storm can wreak havoc with their self-image and sense of self-worth. That is why it is so crucial to teach your children that they are one of a kind, unique and uncomparable to any other human being on earth. Drum into their consciousness the reality of their uniqueness in such a way as to make it become part of the very fabric of their being.

The realization of their uniqueness can be one of the most liberating and empowering discoveries of their lives.

Imagine how free they will feel when they really understand that the only person worth comparing themselves to is themselves. This is one of the most exciting lessons that they can learn from biology and genetics as well.

Each Individual Is Miraculous

Think of it this way—in order for any baby to be born, first the egg of the mother must be fertilized by the sperm of the father. However, we all know that in every ejaculation there are literally millions of sperm, all vying to connect with the same egg. What that means in real life is that every single baby that is conceived starts out from the very beginning of fertilization as the winner of a lottery against far greater odds than any state lottery for money in the history of gambling.

The sperm that fertilized the egg that grew to be you or any one of your children was the one that succeeded against the most incredible odds imaginable. That means that each of us starts out as a winner, an immediate and undeniable success in the race of life. So, too, the individual egg and individual sperm that joined together in unique combination to form each of us was a once-in-history combination, that never occurred in all of recorded time, and will never occur again.

When our children *feel* like the unique, special, extraordinary and wondrous creations that they are, it can only help to bolster their self-pride. Since that is one of our most important parenting goals, it is also why it is so crucial to communicate to each and every one of your children just how exceptional they truly are.

The Self-Fulfilling Prophecy

Children who believe that they are bad shape their actions to fit their view of themselves. This is what has classically been known as the "self-fulfilling prophecy." What it means, simply put, is that whether kids think they are good or they are bad often *makes* it so. In one way or another, all of us unconsciously adjust our behavior to match our inner expectations. We want to be consistent with our self-image, and so we act in whatever way will make us feel more secure, by tuning our behavior to what we think we know about ourselves and how someone "like us" is "supposed" to act in any given situation.

The good news about self-fulfilling prophecies is that they work the same whether the self-image is a good one or a bad one, whether positive or negative. Just as it is so often true that if you think you are bad you will act out in a way that proves you are right (since after all, everyone wants to be right, especially when it comes to themselves), so too if you think and believe that you are good, capable, lovable, and competent, you will act in such a way as to demonstrate that you do indeed possess all of those qualities.

Because of the power of the self-fulfilling prophecy, children who act out in negative ways, often are found to be doing so primarily as a way of matching their behavior to a pre-existing poor self-image. That is why one of the most important jobs that parents have in the raising of their children, is to instill a positive set of expectations as early on as possible in their children's lives. Simply put, positive self-images produce positive, socially acceptable behavior, while negative self-images produce negative, unacceptable behavior.

The Need to Be Acknowledged

In one way or another, along with the impetus of the self-fulfilling prophecy, there is always an aspect of such behavior that is designed to fulfill the basic, fundamental need that all of us have for acknowledgment. Though all kids seek such acknowledgment, they don't all go about it in the same way.

Some kids get the acknowledgment they need by acting good, and others by acting bad. Either way, the end result is the same—kids get attention and one form or another of acknowledgment from adults. What this translates into is that through their behavior, the reaction of the adults around them lets the children know on the most basic, instinctual levels that their existence is recognized in the world. Someone notices them, and therefore they not only exist, but on some level they belong.

As sad as it seems, when children act out in a negative fashion, they are telegraphing the message that they would rather get negative attention than no attention at all. When kids are starved for attention, for affection, for encouragement, for acknowledgment from adults, they will make sure they get that attention in just about any way that they can. Part of our job as parents is to direct their behavior toward positive, nurturing, socially acceptable paths so that we can use their own behavior and actions to reinforce an internal belief that their essential nature is one of goodness and value.

A Self-Esteem Checklist

What is the difference between a child with high self-esteem and a child with low self-esteem? The following is a reasonable checklist to measure your own child's behavior and attitudes:

A CHILD WITH HIGH SELF-ESTEEM*

1. Is proud of his or her accomplishments

2. Can act independently

*Adapted from H. Clemes and R. Bean. *Self-Esteem: The Key to Your Child's Well-Being.* New York: Putnam, 1981.

3. Assumes responsibility

4. Can tolerate frustration

5. Approaches challenges with enthusiasm

6. Feels capable of taking charge of situations in his or her own life

7. Has a good sense of humor

8. Has a sense of purpose

9. Can postpone gratification

10. Seeks help when needed

11. Is confident and resourceful

12. Is active and energetic, and spontaneously expresses his or her feelings

13. Is relaxed and can manage stress

A CHILD WITH LOW SELF-ESTEEM

1. Plays it safe by avoiding situations that require taking risks

2. Feels powerless

3. Becomes easily frustrated

4. Is overly sensitive

5. Constantly needs reassurance

6. Is easily influenced by others

7. Frequently uses the phrase "I don't know" or "I don't care"

8. Is withdrawn

9. Blames others for his or her failures

10. Is isolated, has few friends, is preoccupied

11. Is uncooperative and angry

12. Is uncommunicative

13. Is clingy, dependent

14. Is constantly complaining

15. Has a general negative attitude

The Power of Parent-Talk

In her marvelous book *The Magic of Encouragement,* Stephanie Marston recounts the incredible power that parents' words have on developing either a positive or negative sense of self-worth in their children. She recalls a study by Jack Canfield at the University of Iowa, in which a group of graduate students followed around normal two-year-olds for one day. What they discovered was that these average kids from average families received 432 negative messages (like "Don't touch that . . ." or "You're not big enough to do that . . .") to every 32 positive messages from their parents. At this rate is it any wonder that kids grow up feeling insecure about their own abilities, inadequate to competently negotiate the ups and downs of society, and perhaps even less than totally worthwhile and lovable?

Ms. Marston points out the obvious but important keys to parenting that enhance self-esteem, such as focusing on the behavior and not on the child (note the difference between "You are a bad boy!" and "I don't like it when you throw your clothes all over the floor"), and taking the time to practice building on your child's strengths.

Stealing, lying, fighting, treating others badly—all are the natural outgrowth of children feeling bad about themselves. They may feel rejected by parents, teachers, friends, or family, or jealous and angry at someone close to them. It is important that you do your best to understand the root causes of your children's behavior, so that these can be addressed along with the behavior itself. In fact, it is often easier to remove whatever it is that caused the upset in the first place, than to react with punishments in response to expressions of frustration or anger on the part of your children.

Establish Consequences

Obviously, parents need to set up rules in their homes that will establish clear consequences to the behavior of their children. As we discussed in Chapter 3, children easily learn the difference between punishments and consequences very quickly when simple systems are established and clear expectations spelled out.

Creating clearly understood, and appropriate consequences for behavior is one of the great keys to emotionally healthy children. Consequences need to exist both for positive and negative behavior. As I pointed out previously, too often parents think only of catching their children doing things wrong, so that they can pounce on the misbehavior, "straighten their kids out," and tell them in no uncertain terms exactly how they should be behaving.

Compliment Good Behavior

Without question, however, the most successful parents are those who have their eyes and ears always open to catching their children doing something right. "You only comment about me when I make a mistake or get something wrong," one child told her mother. "How come you never notice it when I do well and get it right?"

Indeed, the child would be much better served if her mother was as vigilant in picking out the correct answers on her school work as she was to find the mistakes. The parent would be eminently more successful if she paid as much attention to the times her daughter did clean her room or her bathroom, or wear clean and nice clothing, as she did to every time something was dirty, or she wore Levis with holes in the knee (which of course happened to be the number one fashion statement on the junior high circuit that year).

Developing the habit of first noticing and then acknowledging the positive attributes of your own children can be one of the most liberating experiences of your parenting career. Very few things are more satisfying or provide a greater feeling of personal worth and importance to children than to have their parents notice the things they do well and then acknowledge them.

In fact, as the world becomes increasingly complex and large, as people feel more and more like tiny dots in an endless sea of humanity and less and less like individuals who truly matter to anyone, the simple attention given by parents to their children which acknowledges their value and worth takes on all the more significance and power.

Notice Your Children

Your children need to know they are loved. They need to know that they are valuable. The need to know that they are important enough for you to take time to be with them individually, to notice what they are doing, how they have dressed, what they have created, how they are growing. Such seemingly small things are more important to the self-esteem of a growing child than most of us ever realize.

Human Mirrors

My experience, after working with people of all ages for many years, is that what most people need above all else in life is a little positive attention. When they get it, whether they are children or adults they respond with pleasure, gratitude, and a heightened sense of self-worth. Of course, all of us on one level or another judge our personal stature and worth on a scale that is created by others. All of us as children watch to see how we are treated by peers, then use this external treatment scale as a gauge to determine whether or not we are "popular."

In a similar way, we watch to see whether our teachers think we are smart or dumb in class. The clues that let us "know" the answer to this question, are how they talk to us, whether or not they call on us for answers to questions, and sometimes whether or not they give us extra work to do or keep us after class.

Everyone uses other people to serve as human mirrors to reflect their own social standing in life. For children, parents are the most important mirror they have. How you treat your children, the tone of voice with which you address them, whether or not you treat them with respect or discount their words, suggestions, and any potential contribution they might make to a conversation, all have a powerful effect on their sense of personal value and self-worth, whether or not you want it to.

That is why parenting is such an awesome responsibility, and why parents so often feel intimidated by all the power that they know they exert over the emotional and spiritual well-being of their children.

The Power of Praise

Every living thing needs sunshine to grow and flourish. Praise, acknowledgment, and positive encouragement are the simple yet powerful ways we bring sunshine into the emotional lives of our children. Never underestimate the power of a parent's approval. Frankly, all you need to do is think about your relationship with your own parents. Somehow, no matter how old we get (and in fact, even after our parents have died), we still feel bad when we experience disapproval or rejection from our parents, and feel better about ourselves when they approve.

Every negative comment is like a rain cloud that washes a bit of self-esteem away. We all know kids who seem to go through life with their own personal thunderstorm hovering over their heads. Most of this can be attributed to the degree to which they have internalized parental disapproval of their behavior, so that they have come to believe that they are inherently bad kids, or failures in life.

One of my favorite stories about how creative each of us, whether parents or teachers, can be when it comes to finding things our children are doing that we can praise, happened in an early childhood classroom. The story concerns a little boy named Adam, who wasn't particularly outstanding at anything in school. However, one day when his mother came to pick him up from school, he was wearing a large gold star pinned to his shirt. His mother was thrilled, and amazed that he had done anything so outstanding as to deserve a gold star, so she hugged him and asked, "Adam, what did you do to earn that wonderful gold star?"

Adam, puffed up with the pride of his accomplishment, replied, "Well, every day we rest, and today *I* rested the best!"

Now *here* was a brilliant teacher. She did what I have been urging you to do all through this book—find something that your child is doing right, and comment on it. Reward desired behavior. It's one of the oldest and most tried and true methods of positive behavior modification ever discovered.

Children as Students of Good Behavior

Of course, it isn't really surprising that parents spend so much time on the negative behavior of their children. If you think about it you will realize that as parents, when after we teach our children what behavior is expected of them, after we tell them "Act like this, but don't act like that," we then expect them to do the right thing naturally. We forget that proper behavior patterns are skills that our children are learning, and that like any skills they only learn by practicing them over and over.

Since we assume proper behavior, we jump on our kids every time they deviate from our expectations. The good behavior goes unacknowledged, since we think that's just the way everyone should act, and it doesn't seem worthy of special notice.

It's important to see your children as if they are merely students of good behavior, with you as their teacher. Just as you wouldn't expect them to master the vocabulary of a foreign language the first, second, or even fifth time they tried, so too it helps to see positive social behavior as a skill that your child is learning. The more positive reinforcement you can give, the better the behavior will be learned. It you looked upon each action that you approved of as a symbol of your child's success, you would find it easier to acknowledge that behavior with a positive verbal comment.

Develop the Habit of Praise

To some parents this may seem like emotional overkill. After all, you are thinking, "If I tell my child to do something, he or she should simply do it. Why should I have to reward my child for simply acting the way he or she ought to act?" We tend to think in this fashion, because we forget that social behavior, whether it is not interrupting another when they are speaking, not throwing things on the floor, saying "Please" or "Thank you," or playing nicely with another child without hitting him or her, all are socially *learned* behaviors. You are your child's primary teacher, and as such want to demonstrate the kind of behavior, including noticing when another person acts correctly, that you want you child to emulate. Give it a try for a week, and I promise you will see such positive, often dramatic results in yourself and your children, that you will quickly develop the habit of daily praise and acknowledgment for all your children.

The Power of Positive Thinking

In 1968, Harvard professors Rosenthal and Jacobson conducted a powerful and revealing experiment into the effects of teacher expectations on the behavior and success of students. This famous study was called the "Pygmalion experiment," and in it they told elementary school teachers that their class had been tested and that certain kids had gifted IQs and others were of average intelligence. What happened was that the children who were labeled gifted did in fact excel in school over those who were labeled average.

The experiment was so powerful because in reality the researchers had simply used the students' locker numbers for their IQ scores. However, since the teachers *thought* they were gifted, they gave them more opportunities and more time to answer questions, called them by name more often, and stepped closer to them and touched them more frequently. All of this extra attention and encouragement added up to these children doing significantly better in school.

So too, with parental expectations. Children often rise or fall with the expectations of the adults who are the significant authority figures in their lives. The famous aphorism "If you think you can or think you can't, you are right" applies equally to the power of your expectations of your children. Treat them like winners, as if you know they will succeed in life and become loving and capable human beings who will be proud of themselves and their accomplishments and who will make you proud to be their parents. Expectations are too often self-fulfilling prophecies, so have faith in your children and their ability to succeed, so that they in turn will have the same faith in themselves.

Find Little Ways to Show You Believe in Them

One of my fondest childhood memories is of lunchtime in elementary school. I assure you it wasn't due to the excellent food in the school cafeteria. Rather, it was because every time I brought my own lunch to school, I would open the bag to discover that my mother had written a note to me and included it along with my lunch. Inevitably the note would tell me that she loved me, that she believed in my abilities to succeed, and that she knew that I would make it a successful day. There are few feelings in life more wonderful than the warm inner glow that comes from knowing that your mother or father is on your side, believes in you, trusts you to succeed, and stands by you through thick and thin.

So, my next suggestion is to do what my mother did. When you send your child off to school, slip a note of positive encouragement in with the lunch. You can never acknowledge your children too much. You can never remind them too often that they are lovable, capable people and that you have faith in them. If you think about your life, you will probably agree that it was the little things, the small gestures of support, encouragement, and love, that have always meant the most to you. Whether it came from your parents, a boy or girl friend, your spouse, partner, or companion, these simple yet heartfelt reminders of their faith in you as a person usually meant more than all the awards of a lifetime.

As a parent, you have the opportunity every single day to give these gifts of the heart to your children. They are simple, and take very little time, yet they can have a powerful impact on their self-esteem and feelings of self-worth and competence that can last them throughout their lives. One thing to remember is that the key to your child's self-esteem lies not in whether or not you love your children, but in whether your children *feel* loved. All the various techniques that I suggest throughout this book are designed to help you create an environment in which your children experience the love that you feel for them, so that they feel worthwhile enough as human beings to be able to give back that love to others.

Daily Filling the Cup of Self-Esteem

One of the most simple yet impactful techniques for accomplishing the emotional reinforcement so necessary to encourage positive self-esteem in your children is to give yourself ethical child-raising "homework" each night. The homework is this—reward your children with *one* positive statement a day. Give them at least one gift each day of acknowledgment. All people, at every age, every social status, every background, every race, every religion, need as much emotional support and nourishment as possible. It is fundamental to the human condition, that we have deep longings for acceptance, acknowledgment, and recognition of our inherent worth and value as human beings. One of the single most important jobs that you have as a parent, is to ensure that your children experience themselves as precious human beings.

There is really little in your life that is more important than this particular parenting task. It takes patience and time, day after day, hour after hour, year after year of conscious attention to the messages that you are giving both verbally and indirectly to your children.

One of the easiest ways of keeping tabs on how well you are reinforcing your children's self-esteem and feelings of self-worth each day, is to ask yourself the question, "If it were up to what I have said and done today, how would my children feel about themselves as human beings? What have I done today to fill their cup of self-esteem so high it begins to overflow?" As you honestly answer the question each day, you will be providing yourself with a built-in guide for establishing the kind of relationship and personal parenting style that accomplishes the self-esteem goals that you have for your children.

Now we turn to the next chapter, and share ideas and techniques for helping your children in the difficult and challenging area of making ethical choices. Together we will explore the idea of creating a shared vision of ethical behavior with them, the importance of team parenting, and the crucial role that demonstrating moral courage can play in your children's lives.

Seven

Making Ethical Choices: Vision and Moral Modeling

The most difficult job our kids have today is learning good conduct without seeing any.
H. G. Hutchinson

Every single day of our lives, we are constantly making decisions that help determine the very nature of our character. Every ethical decision we make, every choice we embrace in our relationships with others becomes part and parcel of our core understanding of our essential nature.

That is why one of the keys to raising ethical, responsible children lies in your ability to communicate to them that the quality of their lives is ultimately dependent upon the quality of their choices. They choose their friends, they choose their behavior, they choose the consequences of their actions, they choose whether to study and do well in school or ditch classes and pay the price. What makes this so important is that the same is true for every aspect of their lives. Ultimately, the nature of their choices determines the quality of their lives.

Quality of Choice = Quality of Life

The power of their daily choices to determine not only the quality of their lives, but its longevity as well, is easily recognized from even a glance at the prevailing statistics concerning how Americans treat their bodies, and the ever-growing use of drugs of all kinds throughout our society. This isn't so much an issue merely of education, of sharing the facts about the impact of drugs on the body. If it was, no one would be smoking cigarettes anymore since it's been over a quarter of a century since the first Surgeon General's report came out directly linking cigarette smoking with cancer, lung disease, heart disease, and a whole host of life-reducing and life-threatening illnesses.

People know about the damage that smoking cigarettes does to their bodies, yet they continue to smoke at alarming rates. According to a U.S. Surgeon General's report, some 52 million Americans smoke an average of 31 cigarettes a day, and between 390,000 and 500,000 people die each year as a direct result of smoking. That's 17.4 percent of all the deaths in the United States. If these statistics are true, then in the next two weeks as many people will die as a direct result of smoking cigarettes as died from AIDS in the United States in 1988.*

This is why I can't overemphasize the importance of teaching your children the impact that their daily choices make on their lives. Choices determine not only who we are, but whether or not we live to see tomorrow. A graphic story in *U.S. News & World Report* (February 6, 1989) claimed that Americans consume more illegal drugs than all the other 5 billion people on the earth. The magazine reported the shocking statistic that over 9 million Americans have tried cocaine; 25 million are involved with illegal drugs of some kind; and 10 percent of the babies born today have been exposed to drugs or high levels of alcohol in the womb.

The same problems exist when it comes to the use of alcohol. The *Dallas Morning News* (March 18, 1988) ran a story in which it reported that approximately 100,000 ten- and eleven-year-olds got drunk at least once every week, that over 100 million Americans drink on a regular basis, and 18.5 million have serious drinking problems. The number of teenage alcoholics was estimated to be 2.5 million.

With the reality behind all of these graphic statistics staring us in the face day in and day out in our own communities and our own families, it shouldn't be difficult to realize why I am making such a strong case for teaching your children the incredible impact that their choices have every single day on the quality of their lives. It is in their

*Zig Ziglar. *Raising Positive Kids in a Negative World*. New York: Ballantine Books, 1989, p. 200.

power to make positive, responsible, appropriate decisions that will make them worthy of your trust and confidence. Empowering them to embrace the challenge of this responsibility for how their own lives will turn out is one of the greatest demands that parenthood places upon all of us.

Choice Not Instinct

Teaching your children how to make responsible ethical decisions involves training them from the earliest years to recognize that all behavior involves choices. In fact, implied in the litany of frightening statistics that I just shared with you is the lesson that the choices themselves determine whether our actions are ethical or not.

Were we to have no choice but, like other animals, to react solely on the basis of instinct, then the entire subject of ethical behavior would be moot. No one holds others to be morally responsible for their behavior if they are seen to be without choice. It is through the choices we make each day in our interactions with others that we define ourselves as moral, ethical beings.

This is why as a parent it is so important to create opportunities for your children to recognize their ability to make choices, and understand and experience the consequences of those choices. Even when they are young, your children can be given a wide range of choices over their own lives. "Do you want to wear the blue shirt or the green shirt today?" "Do you want to walk or ride?" "Do you want to eat it now or later?" "Do you want to eat the banana or the apple?" All of these are age-appropriate decisions that will give your children the necessary training in making daily decisions that affect their lives. You start with the simple and harmless choices, so that as they grow older they will be competent to make the more difficult and potentially dangerous choices as well.

When children grow up habituated to making choices for themselves, they learn the importance of respecting the rights of others to make choices as well. In addition, giving your children real choices throughout their lives empowers them to feel that they have some control over both themselves and the world around them. This too is a crucial component of ethical behavior—the recognition that each of us has an impact on the world in which we live through the choices that we make.

Empowering your children with the ability to make choices and the understanding of the consequences of those choices on their lives and the lives of those with whom they interact also adds to their sense of growing responsibility toward others in the larger social structure. This realization also strengthens your children's feelings of being irrefutably connected to the lives of other human beings, which in turn, reinforces in a positive and nurturing way the understanding that each of us is both autonomous and independent while remaining connected and interdependent.

Modeling Ethical Decisions at Home

Since your family is a kind of self-contained social structure, and since (as I keep reminding you), your primary challenge is to constantly model for your children the adults you want them to grow up to be, it is helpful to look upon rule-making as just another opportunity for training them in the art of ethical decision making. To accomplish this, rather than continuing to foster the traditional autocratic "all decisions are made by parents" model of family interactions, you might try creating a model that is more democratic, more empowering for your children, and more respectful of them as individuals with their own thoughts, ideas, and concerns.

The direct approach to democracy at home involves simply including your children in the decision-making process when it comes to rules. You'll be surprised at how thoughtful and appropriate their rules will most likely be, and how much easier it is to get them to follow the house rules when they have had a hand in creating them in the first place.

Rules Are a Two-Way Street

There is one small aspect of the democratic approach, however, to which parents often have the most resistance. When rules are openly and democratically arrived at with the input of both adults and children, *both* adults and children must abide by them as well. One of the key differences in this system is that parents are bound by the rules as much as children, wherever it is appropriate.

For example, if the entire family is involved in the setting up of rules relating to the household chores that must be done, or how much television will be watched in the house during a given week, both adults and children must be respectful of the decisions. When you demonstrate respect for joint decisions, you teach your children integrity, that keeping one's word is important, and that you respect and value their input and ideas.

There are many everyday areas of individual and family life in which your children can have input when it comes to rules, standards of behavior, expectations, and decisions. Some of those areas include recreational times, recreational activities, study hours, study habits (can they study with the radio playing or their favorite CDs as background music?), what they eat at meals, whom they spend non-school time with, clothing that they wear, how they spend their own money, household chores they must do, attendance at church or synagogue, participation in extracurricular activities, or how often each month a friend can spend the night, or they can go overnight to a friend's house.

Each of these and hundreds more decisions each year can be made much more effectively if your children have an active, serious part in the establishment of the household rules. In this way behavior is less likely to become reduced to acting out in ways designed to challenge your parental authority and establish their independence and maturity level. Your children will know that they are considered responsible and mature because they were included from the start in a democratic decision-making process, and they will subsequently have a greater emotional stake in keeping the rules intact and abiding by them.

Family Meetings

Many families have regularly scheduled "family meetings," once a week, twice a month, or at whatever interval works best for them. During these meetings family issues are discussed respectfully with one another; rules are reviewed to see how they are working and whether anyone has a particular problem keeping them; plans and decisions are made for future activities and family events; responsibilities are shared and assigned so that each family member agrees to his or her particular area of activity and responsibility; and complaints and concerns are aired and worked out.

These meetings have no particular set format that works for everyone. Instead, individual families work out the method that best suits their particular needs, the personalities involved, and the kinds of issues that they will confront. The key is to encourage maximum participation by all members of the family. In that way, everyone feels that their concerns are being heard and dealt with (even if the resolution isn't always to everyone's full satisfaction), and that they are important within the family system and are taken seriously. Further, excellent lessons in conflict resolution, democratic negotiation, and compromise are learned in a safe, supportive environment.

It is important to remember that your family has its own unique life rhythm and set of relationships and expectations, and is a form of culture all its own. It is a kind of "mini-society," and as such ideally ought to reflect the ethical principles and ideals that you would want your children to emulate outside the home, and when they, too, become adults.

Music, Culture, and Ethical Decisions

No one really knows exactly what influence popular music has on how kids view the world or the lifestyle choices that they make. It has engendered fierce debate for decades, with one generation claiming that the moral fiber of the next generation is being eroded by the constant bombardment of music with lyrics that glorify violence, sex, drugs, suicide, infidelity, and the like. Without jumping into the fray on one side or the other, I do believe that there is some logic to the idea that since we do on some level become what we think about, the more we can help fill our children's minds with positive, caring, compassionate, nurturing, inspiring thoughts, the more naturally and automatically they will become individuals who exhibit those very qualities and characteristics.

By the same token, helping our children to identify the negative messages in song lyrics, movies, and the like will to some degree help mitigate their negative effect. This is by no means a trivial issue when you consider the fact that between the seventh and twelfth grades, the average teenager listens to something like 10,500 hours of rock music. It's only about 500 hours less than the total time he or she spends in twelve years of school.

Be a Visionary Guide

One of the most important roles you can play in your child's moral development is to be a visionary guide. You can encourage your children to create in their own minds a vision or picture of the ethical being they wish to become. This is a powerful technique which you can teach your children, for it helps them first to form a general picture or vision regarding what an ethical, caring, compassionate, moral person looks, talks, and acts like, and then to personalize that vision into a positive model of the ethical being they wish to grow up to be.

The greatest philosophers and theologians of every era have recognized the fundamental truth that we become what we think about. "As you think, so shall you become," has been the best selling motto of countless psychological self-help groups, teachers, and motivational materials for decades. In the Biblical book of Proverbs (23:7) we are taught, "For as one thinks, so shall his (sic) end be." For nearly 4,000 years, this simple truth about the power of thought, of internalizing the qualities, values, goals, and images that we wish to emulate and express in our own lives has been a driving force behind successful men and women in all fields of endeavor.

The challenge of successful ethical parenting is to help guide your children along this path of positive self-imaging for the future, so that the picture they create and nurture within represents the highest, brightest, noblest, most caring, and most compassionate picture of an ethical self that they can possibly create.

Some Practical Hints for Parents

Now I want to share some practical hints for parents on how to utilize your own childhood experiences to maximize your clarity and effectiveness in parenting your own children. First, take the time to create a clear picture of the parenting models that most profoundly and directly affected your life as a child. Recognize that the natural tendency of human beings is to unconsciously imitate the models with which we grow up. Therefore, as parents, husbands, and wives, it is crucial to identify as clearly as you can exactly which role models influenced your own perceptions of what it means to be a parent.

Picture your own father, mother, stepparent, or other significant adult "parenting" role model from within your own childhood. Perhaps it was a grandparent who most profoundly influenced your life, who subconsciously serves today as your primary role model; perhaps it was an aunt or uncle, or even an older brother or sister who was placed in a parenting role with you due to the circumstances of your life.

How would you describe them as parents? Take a few moments to do the following simple exercise that will help clarify exactly how you do perceive these significant parenting models in your life.

1. List five qualities that represent their parenting style (autocratic and domineering, supportive and nurturing, democratic and open, and so forth).

2. List three outstanding examples of typical parenting interactions that you recall from your childhood relationship with them.

3. If you could have changed them in any way, what would you have changed?

4. If you could have told them anything as a child that you wanted them to do, or say, what would it have been?

5. Recall a time you told yourself as a child, "When I'm a mother/father, I'll *never* do that," and see if in fact you do it now.

6. If you could, what would you change about your own parenting today?

7. Recall your three most positive memories of interactions as a child with your parents. Identify the qualities that they exhibited that helped make those experiences so powerful and positive for you.

The "Ideal" Parent

When I used to travel the country leading teacher-training workshops for religious school teachers, one of the most important issues that they consistently raised was the problem loosely referred to as "classroom management." Teachers in every setting seem to find managing the classroom environment—getting kids to do what they are supposed to do and creating an environment that encourages the best in children—to be their greatest challenge.

The Ideal Teacher

One of the most successful and effective techniques that I developed to help teachers over the years was an exercise I called the "Ideal Teacher." In it, teachers were asked to see in their mind's eye one of the most positive and influential teachers in their own life experience. It could have been someone from any grade level, at any time in their own student career from elementary education through adult learning experiences, as long as it was a positive teaching role model.

I would then ask them to list five of the qualities that in their minds, based on their own personal experiences, contributed to those teachers' being so outstanding. In all the years of doing this exercise, never once did anyone find this an impossible task. Everyone has had at least one positive teacher in their lives, and everyone could list the qualities that to them made that teacher outstanding.

After the participants created their personal list of outstanding teacher qualities, I would have them share with the total group and list them all on the board in front of the workshop. In the end, we would have a giant composite list of all the qualities that make teachers outstanding, based on real human beings.

After discussing each of the qualities, and allowing the teachers to share what it was about those qualities that they felt made them important for the "ideal teacher," I always encouraged them to write them down on signs and put them up on the walls of their own classrooms. In this way they would surround their own teaching environment with constant reminders of the qualities that they already know they would like to emulate and exhibit in their own lives.

You Too Know the Secret

I share this powerful teacher-training process with you in this book on parenting, because I truly believe that you, too, already know the secret. After years of working with parents of all kinds and backgrounds, helping them work through a wide variety of parenting issues and challenges, I have come to believe that each of us has the ability to draw upon our own experiences of how our parents affected us, to create our own picture of the "Ideal Parent" as well.

When it comes to parenting, as it is with teaching (which of course is often referred to as *in loco parentis*, "in place of a parent"), by using your own life and personal experiences as your primary reference point, you can identify both positive and negative examples of parenting behavior from which you can learn. It can often be just as important to learn what not to do from your personal parenting models as it is learning what to do.

Create a concrete, usable picture of your "Ideal Parent" in the same way I used to have teachers create the "Ideal Teacher." Begin by examining your own life experiences as a child, looking for both the positive and negative aspects of your own parents' behavior and the impact that their parenting choices and behavior had on you. List as many positive examples of parenting behaviors and decisions as you can, followed by a brief (one line) note as to the positive result that this behavior had in your own life.

If you are married, this can be a wonderful activity to do with your spouse. Each of you had different parenting role models, and each of you has a lifetime of valuable experiences to share with each other, as a way of helping create your own unique parenting team together.

Team Parenting

One of the keys to successful parenting is to approach it as a team. Both parents need to agree upon how they will react to their children's behavior. Both need to agree upon the guidelines and boundaries of acceptable behavior and the consequences for misbehavior. Just as the ideal marriage is a team marriage, so too the ideal parenting approach is one based upon the team model.

Parenting is a partnership between all parents. Whether there are one, two, three, or four parents involved in the family sphere of your child's experience, it is best for the child if you all cooperate and function as partners. I realize that this is often not possible, given the intensity of feelings leading to and following the breakup of marriage relationships. Even so, ideally the child's welfare ought to out-weigh the individual hurts and angers that divorced parents feel toward each other and give them a common focus around which they can put personal feelings aside.

To the degree that you can function as a team of parenting partners, your child's emotional, spiritual, and moral upbringing will be strengthened. In fact, often it is the absence of parents acting as a team, agreeing upon the consequences of behavior and the expectations of ethical choices, that lies at the root of children's discipline problems.

When Parents Have Differing Values

Children need to have a clear understanding of what is expected of them in all aspects of their lives. It is especially true when it comes to ethical behavior. When one parent acts with obvious concern, sensitivity, and compassion toward those less fortunate, and the other speaks of them as criminals, or "low lifes," who got what they deserved and should be run out of town, it is obvious that the child will suffer from an ethical identity crisis.

Children need a consistent set of ethical guidelines to follow, with consistent behavioral expectations that they understand. When they don't know which parent to listen to, which parent to follow, which parent is "right," because they are receiving mixed messages, it stands to reason that they will be mixed up, too. If you are divorced, do your best to have a conference with your ex-spouse about the ethical upbringing of your child. If need be, enlist the aid of a counselor, clergy person or mutual friend to act as go-between or mediator, so that hopefully you can agree upon a set of expectations and standards of behavior that will be consistent.

176 Raising Ethical Children

Finding Agreement

Agreeing in this way may be one of the greatest and most
loving gifts you can give to your children. It can save them
from a tremendous amount of emotional turmoil, confusion, and suffering. There are a few relatively simple steps
that you can take to help you arrive at a program of agreed-
upon expectations and behavioral consequences.

First, sit down and have this conference. Individually
make a list of the behaviors that are important to both of
you, both those you expect and want, and those of which
you disapprove and don't want. Then compare your lists
and edit them together into a third document that enu-
merates all those points about which you agree. This will
leave only those about which you disagree to discuss,
clarify, and work out with the help of your outside friend,
clergy person, or counselor.

Second, do the same for the list of consequences for
undesirable behavior. Ideally your children will experience
the same repercussions for their behavior regardless of the
home in which they happen to be at a given moment. In
that way the messages about ethical behavior are clear;
your children learn a consistent set of rules and have a
much greater sense of emotional security and inner peace.
Otherwise, you are opening the door to increased psychological stress and confusion, and placing your children in
the position of having to constantly juggle a confusing
entanglement of moral codes and ethical expectations.

Presenting a Clear and Consistent Message

Just as successful marriages depend on creating a team
marriage, so too, successful parenting depends on creating
a team approach in as many areas as possible. Either as a
child or a parent, nearly everyone has had the experience

of children trying to play one parent off against the other, telling one that the other said it was OK to do something, then going to the other and repeating the story in reverse.

Successful parenting requires a successful team so that your children will receive clear and consistent messages. Your children need the security of knowing that both (or hopefully, *all* if there are divorces and remarriages) of their parents have a coordinated, supportive, and consistent approach to parenting. Being able to play one parent off against the other, to manipulate parents into giving in on important decisions, and knowing that one's parents have no clear and consistent parenting guidelines, promotes insecurity and even anger in children.

Children need to know that their parents' values are consistent, that they can be counted on time and again, and that the family world in which they are being raised has a clear set of family values that can be articulated and easily identified. In the insecure, ever-changing world of childhood, having consistent and clear values upon which your children can rely is one of the most important spiritual and emotional gifts that you can give them.

Nurture Awareness of Self

Another important method for helping your children to focus on their own ethical behavior and choices is to remind them to take the time to stop and *think* about their behavior before acting. Most kids, most of the time, simply act, without examining their actions in advance. To lead a self-consciously aware ethical life, however, our children must learn the skill of stepping away emotionally from their own actions so that they can look at them more objectively and make intelligent choices regarding whether or not they wish to repeat those specific acts.

This ability to create an emotional distance from one's self, to intellectually step outside oneself and examine one's own behavior is an important skill that only comes with practice. This, too, children can learn by the example of their parents. If they see their parents uniformly justifying their own actions, always defending every decision they make even if they actually have thought better of it later, then the children learn that "circling your wagons" and never admitting you are wrong is the highest virtue.

It is far better for children to hear their parents rethink hasty decisions that they might have expressed out loud, and see that the adults whom they love and respect have the capacity to admit mistakes, to change their minds, and to examine choices and behavior from an objective nondefensive position. Although admittedly not always an easy thing to do, this is the best way to teach your children an important lesson about humility and moral self-examination.

There is ample evidence to show that kids who think about and discuss openly moral issues and moral choices make much better progress through the various stages of moral development than those who don't. So encourage your kids to talk about the important issues of their lives, by creating an environment within your home in which they hear you speak about the things that are important to you in your life.

Teach Your Kids That They Do Make a Difference

One of the keys to raising ethical children is to teach them that they do make a difference in the world. Ethical people feel empowered to affect their lives and the lives of others. They have generally grown up with parents who were good role models of individuals who lived by their own moral standards and ideals.

"Love" and "respect" go hand in hand at every level of child raising. In fact, you might say that if a child doesn't feel respected by his or her parents as an individual, he or she will not truly feel loved either. Demonstrating to your children that they are worthy of your respect—by listening to them when they talk, by encouraging them to make suggestions and give opinions on important issues, by sometimes (but not all the time) changing your way of doing something after listening to their suggestions and ideas, by giving them your attention and your time—is probably the most important spiritual, intellectual, ethical gift you can give them as they are growing up.

In *Positive Social Behavior and Morality*, Vol. 2, Ervin Staub tells us that studies indicate that young people who stand up for their own rights and the rights of others come from families that encourage independence and self-expression. He demonstrated in his own research that before kids can take seriously their own moral decisions and ethical priorities, they must first respect themselves and see themselves as valuable and worthy of expressing opinions and being involved with making decisions about the fate of the world.

Creating an Open Climate

If you want your kids to feel free to discuss difficult moral issues with you (which you do), then you have to start young in creating an open, positive, nonjudgmental, safe climate in which to struggle out loud with such issues. If everytime your child says something with which you disagree, you immediately interject, "That's stupid!" or "Where did you learn that garbage?" or "That's a ridiculous thing to say," you will be teaching your child that it's safer not to offer opinions in the first place.

No one likes to be called "stupid," and no one likes to feel stupid either. Few of us are willing more than once or twice to put ourselves in situations where our egos are being attacked, and our self-respect is under fire. We would much rather just back out of the whole discussion, and find a "safer" topic to discuss.

Encourage Discussion

That is why it is so important for you to go out of your way to encourage discussion, encourage disagreement, encourage diversity of opinion within your family. It is really the only healthy way to arrive at a clearer moral position on the difficult and complex ethical issues that abound in our society. The more we struggle out loud with others about these issues, the more clearly we can define and redefine our beliefs and standards of ethical behavior. This process is an important part of the methodology through which you can train your children to grapple with serious moral issues.

Some families use the dinner table as a time to bring up moral issues that are part of their lives. Others use stories from the newspapers or the "Dear Abby" columns to provide safe and nonthreatening grist for the ethical dilemmas mill. In discussing such real-life dramas as the newspapers can provide, you are turning your dining room into an ethics laboratory, and allowing your children to be co-partners with the adults in the process of moral discovery and decision making.

Become an Island of Safety and Support

Ideally, your family can become a safe island of support, acceptance, respect, and love in an often harsh and uncompromising world. It can serve as the permanent "safe house" for moral questions, debate, and struggle. After all, wouldn't you rather have your children grappling with difficult ethical choices involving drugs, sex, interpersonal relationships, abortion, individual choice, personal freedom, and the like in your home, with you and your family, than to have the only place they feel safe to talk about these tough moral issues be in their friends' homes with their parents?

Ultimately you have to ask yourself the question, "If my kid's values don't come from me and what I am teaching them, where will they come from?" The answer, unfortuately, is that they will come from the popular media of the day. The primary ethical training of your children will be left to whatever situations, ideas, and stories the writers and producers of daily sitcoms, soap operas, and other popular television shows happen to put on the air. If you don't take firm charge of your child's ethical upbringing, you are leaving it in the hands of television, radio, movies, popular music, and friends. You *must* assert your role and responsibility as primary moral teacher and guide of your children, or else you abdicate your moral responsibility as parent. Then your children grow up in a moral vacuum, to be filled by whatever stranger happens to pass by.

You must believe that you have an important moral and ethical message to pass on to your children. You must believe that the ethical values that underlie the foundation of Western society are good, worthwhile, positive, correct, and crucial to the fulfillment of our social and political dreams for the future.

Expressing Moral Courage

It takes moral courage to be a parent today. It takes moral courage to accept the awesome responsibility of raising children in what so often appears to be an unhealthy, unethical moral climate. It takes moral courage to believe in yourself and your standards of behavior, to believe that there are fundamental values that transcend time and popularity and that are worth being passionate about with your children.

It even takes courage in this day and age to openly embrace any religious outlook on life, whatever that religion may be, and to teach that religious perspective to your children. Yet, year after year, the individuals with the strongest sense of morality and ethics, with the strongest and most solid ethical foundation upon which to meet the trials and tribulations, challenges and complex ethical demands of today, are those whose spiritual and religious foundations are strong.

It doesn't matter so much *which* religion is embraced, only that *a* religion is embraced. Ultimately, regardless of the claims of one religious group or another to have the "right answer," or to be in special direct contact with God and God's will, all religions have the same ultimate goal— to create moral, ethical, caring, compassionate, passionate, committed human beings. I believe that at the base of all religions the ultimate goal of their rituals, customs, holidays, theological teachers, prayers, songs, and sacred texts is to help us to be the best human beings that we can possibly be, so that we can create an earth filled with Godliness, justice, and compassion.

All religions teach a reverence for life; that life is sacred; that we are all part of one universal human family with common dreams, common desires, common visions of the future world that we must create together. All human beings are in search of meaning, purpose, spiritual fulfillment, and nourishment. And all of Western society is based on a common set of spiritual values that each of us wants to pass on to our children—integrity, honesty, justice, compassion, forgiveness, humility, personal growth, respect, love.

Making Ethical Behavior Ordinary

An ancient Hebrew proverb teaches that "the highest form of wisdom is kindness." After over two decades of counseling individuals and families and watching parents struggling to pass on ethical values and a strong moral foundation to their children amidst all the countervailing undermining stresses and forces of our modern "look-out-for-number-one" society, I am more convinced than ever of the power of this simple value to change people's lives. Showing kindness to another human being, especially your own child on a consistent basis is one of the single most powerful parenting gifts you could possibly give.

What makes simple kindness such a powerful tool? It communicates clearly on a direct emotional level that you believe in the inherent worth and value of the person to whom the kindness is directed. It therefore makes the other person feel important, valuable, and worthy of being cared about. Showing kindness to other human beings, especially your own children, also serves to clearly demonstate on a daily basis that positive ethical values can be expressed in your everyday life. It doesn't take a special event, extraordinary accomplishment, or unusual set of circumstances for ethical behavior to be practiced.

Ordinary Behavior as Ethical Behavior

What you want to teach your children is that when it comes to ethical behavior, making moral choices takes place each and every day of their lives. Since you are their primary caregiver, you are also their primary ethical influence, and only you have the opportunity each day to demonstrate what I call the "ordinariness" of high ethical expectations.

You want your children to take ethical behavior in stride, to see it as simply an ordinary aspect of their everyday lives. You don't want them to grow up thinking that demonstrating ethical behavior is something that only happens under great duress, or in times of unusual circumstances (like watching those ethical action heroes on television who pulled individuals away from the rioting mobs to safety during the Los Angeles riots of 1992).

Ethical behavior, to be fundamental to your children's character, must be integrated into their everyday lives. It must be found in the simple gestures, the offhand remarks, the casual almost unconscious acts of kindness and concern, that are natural reflections of their fundamental attitudes toward other human beings. The road to such a firm ethical foundation lies not only in pointing out the unusual acts of ethical bravery or heroism, but in the daily, simple, ordinary ethical actions that occur between one family member and another, one friend and another, or one stranger and another.

More Teachable Moments

When one of your children volunteers to help a younger sibling with homework, when your child goes over to a sick friend's house for a visit, when someone in your family does something nice for another without being asked or expecting anything special in return, *these* are the teachable moments of ethical behavior. These are the everyday opportunities to give praise and acknowledgment for bringing more kindness, caring, and love into the world.

Others may disagree, but I believe that you can never give a child too much acknowledgment or positive reinforcement for the ethical acts of their everyday lives. After all, opportunities for unusual heroism are rare, but oppor-

tunities for everyday heroism are just that, everyday opportunities for ethical greatness.

The Small Print of Life

Teach your children that greatness lies not in the splashy
headlines of life, but in the small print—not just in coming
through in the rare moments of extraordinary crisis, but in
being there for others in the simple, ordinary moments of
their everyday lives. Your children learn this lesson, only if
you take the time to point out the ethical implications of
their actions and the actions of others with whom they
interact.

Point out how they feel when a kindness is done to
them. Point out how they feel when someone goes out of
their way to help them with a difficult problem, or make
them feel more comfortable in a new social situation.
These are the kinds of ethical behaviors that are available
to everyone every day. That is why it is so important for you
to call them to the attention of your children as examples
of what it means to live life as a caring, responsible, ethical
human being.

No one was ever made an ethical human being solely by
being taught how to read, write, do math, or conduct scientific experiments. If we learned anything during the
twentieth century about ethical behavior as a species, it is
that intellectual knowledge, scientific brilliance, or academic competence has very little if anything at all to do
with determing the ethical nature of an individual or
society. If that were true, the horrors of the Holocaust, the
brutal degradation of millions of human beings by others
who were well-educated, intellectually sophisticated, and
academically erudite, could never have taken place!

Unfortunately, we have been taught over and over again,
that mere intellectual knowledge is no hedge against emotional brutality. Only when we reward our children for acts

of kindness in the same ways that we reward them for an outstanding grade in math, will we really have a chance of creating a society based on compassion, justice, and ethical righteousness.

Studies of altruistic behavior during the Holocaust in Europe showed that those individuals who risked their own lives to protect others, who took children into their homes to hide them from the Nazis, or set up secret schools, provided food and clothing for the oppressed, by and large never thought they were doing anything extraordinary at all. They consistently reported to those who studied such behavior that they simply couldn't imagine acting in any other way. To them, such behavior was the everyday, ordinary expression of what it means to be a human being in society with other human beings who have similar hopes, dreams, and needs.

The Power of Parental Example

Such individuals learned that this behavior was "ordinary" primarily from the examples of their own parents and how they treated other people, and secondarily from the lessons they learned from compassionate and caring ministers and priests in the religious institutions to which they belonged. *First* came an ethical home life, which was then reinforced by the formal ethical teachings of their religious training.

That is why being conscious of the everyday opportunities to reinforce ethical behavior by your own actions is so crucial to raising ethical children. Time and again the fundamental truth of the power of personal parental example is underscored by the testimony of caring ethical people. We cannot always know what our children are experiencing *outside* our homes, but we do have some measure of control over what happens *inside*. Our homes must be sanctuaries of safety, as well as laboratories for nurturing, warm, loving relationships. When our children feel loved for who they are and not only for their external accomplishments, they will be better able to love themselves, and in turn show love for others.

When they know what it feels like on a daily basis to be shown kindness, consideration, respect, and dignity by parents and siblings, they will in turn express those same qualities and exhibit those same characteristics toward others as a matter of course. The idea is to create an ethical context for their lives such that they really can't imagine living with people in any other way. That is what I mean by the power of making ethical behavior ordinary, and it is one of the most important challenges for parents whose desire is to raise caring, compassionate, and ethical children.

Now we will turn to the issue of peers and friendships and how they will ultimately affect the ethical decisions with which your children will inevitably be confronted.

Eight

Peers, Friendships, and Ethical Decisions

We must teach our children to dream with their eyes open.

Harry Edwards

I don't think I have ever met a parent in all my years who didn't on some level yearn for the ability to pick their children's friends. "Why do they continue to stay friends with Susan (or John, or Sheila, or Sam or . . .)," they lament, "when it constantly seems to cause them nothing but upset, irritation, and pain?" Parents find themselves forever comforting their children, drying their tears of frustration or anger as they suffer the slings and arrows of outrageous friendships, and wondering if there will ever be an end to the pain that ill-conceived peer relationships seem to foster.

Modeling Friendship

Unfortunately, parents can't choose their kids' friends for them. But that doesn't mean that there is nothing of value that you can do to influence the type and quality of your children's friendships. I believe there is! In fact, though you can't actually handpick your children's friends, there is one thing that you can do that is probably even more important than that for your children—you can choose your own friends!

One of the powerful ways that you can use your own life to serve as a model for your children and the values that you want to pass on to them is to pay attention to the kind of friends with whom you surround yourself. Make your friendships models for your children. Have the kind of friends, and more importantly *be* the kind of friend to others that you would want your children to be for their friends. As with every ethical decision that your children will be making in life, the choice of whom they have as friends, the kind of people with whom they are comfortable, the various ways in which they relate to their friends, all will have a profound impact on the kinds of ethical decisions that they will be making on a day-to-day basis.

To realize just how impactful decisions regarding peers can be in a young person's life, think back to the impact that your own friends had on your life as a child growing up. As you grew and matured, you probably went through periods of time in which the approval of your friends was more important to you than the approval or disapproval of your parents, teachers, or siblings. In fact, throughout much of your growing years, the very yardstick by which you would most often judge your own behavior, measure your success or failure as a person, was that of peer acceptance or rejection. If a certain behavior, use of speech, activity, or even article of clothing was acceptable or "cool" as far as your friends were concerned, then it would be desirable to you as well.

Of course this social reality of childhood is a constant source of concern and at times outright fear for parents of all socioeconomic levels, races, and religions. Parents lament their inability to overcome the powerful pressure that peers exert on their children, in so many diverse areas of their lives. When all is said and done, however, regardless of how you personally feel about it, it is one of the realities of life as a parent that you will simply have to accept.

Don't Try to Dictate Friendships

The bad news is that you can't eliminate the influence that peers will have on your children altogether, but the good news is that you still can have at least a subtle influence on the choice of peers themselves. No, I am not suggesting that if you disapprove of one of your son's friends, you simply march into his bedroom and announce that "From now on, you are no longer allowed to have Michael as your friend." Having been there myself as a child, I can tell you that ninety-nine percent of the time, it simply doesn't work.

In fact, when as a young boy my parents disapproved of one of my friends, and told me that they didn't want me to spend time with him, it simply made being with him more of a challenge and much more attractive than it otherwise might have been.

"Michael" and I became very creative at devising opportunities to play together, and "Jimmy" and I went so far as to sneak out of the house at 3 A.M., hop on our bikes in the dead of night, meet on an agreed-upon corner halfway between our homes, and then ride to an all-night restaurant to share an exciting, clandestine early morning breakfast. Knowing that it was an outrageous thing to do and that our parents would hit the ceiling if they ever found out was half the fun.

Jimmy and I stayed friends for life, but I soon lost interest in Michael. I share this story to point out that some things are beyond a parent's control, and other things are not. Trying to dictate friendships to your children will most likely be nothing more than an exercise in futility. Better to pay attention to the rest of this book, model the kind of ethical behavior in the rest of your life that you want your children to emulate, and then trust that they will ultimately make the right decisions.

The fact is that as parents we don't always know which friends are the "right" friends, and which are not. You may remember the wonderful Eddie Haskel character on "Leave It to Beaver," who always appeared to be such a polite, sweet, compliant, and thoughtful young man to Beaver's parents, but was quite the opposite when left alone with his peers. That's why your influence on the friendships of your children will be mostly indirect, rather than obvious and direct. It will happen in the moments when they turn to you for advice on how to deal with a girlfriend or boyfriend, or how to handle jealousy they might be experiencing regarding the looks, affluence, or accomplishments of their friends.

When you raise your children with the values that are important to you—to see the world through the lenses of your ethical system—it becomes incumbent upon you to trust their judgment in the end as well. Most of the time you won't be disappointed, and they will rise to the occasion, particularly when you have clearly articulated the values and ethical standards to which you aspire as a family.

In my counseling experience with many families, most of the time the relationships that parents disapprove of eventually die out of their own accord. Children are perceptive enough, conscious enough, enough aware of the true nature of their friends, to make decisions that serve their ultimate best interests, even at the price of eventually dropping some of their peers from their list of friends.

Social Engineering

The best way to influence the choices of your children when it comes to choosing friends is to do your best to arrange for them to be in situations where the kind of kids whom they will come in contact with will generally be the kind you'd like them to have as friends.

For example, if you encourage your children to get involved with afterschool activities of an athletic, cultural, social, or religious nature, it is much more likely that they will naturally form friendships with other kids who are also part of those same groups. Susan plays in a local soccer league, and her best friends end up being kids who are on her team. What they share is a healthy organized outlet for their physical energy, in an environment that inherently promotes good values such as working with others, good sportspersonship, learning the importance of putting in the time needed to excel at the skills necessary to play the game, and learning how to be a good loser when things don't go their way.

Sam participates in the local church youth group, and loves the community action projects that the group sponsors, like visiting a local homeless shelter to serve dinner once a month, and singing for people in a convalescent home. Naturally, the kids that become Sam's friends are also part of the same church group, who then share common ethical values and an approach to being involved in the lives of others that strongly meets with your approval as parents.

This is by far the most effective way to subtly influence the friendship choices of your children. I like to call it "social engineering" of the best sort, since until late adolescence, you can still have some sway over the extracurricular activities that your kids embrace. Go out of your way to encourage the kind of activities you admire, and discourage those you don't. If you would rather have your daughter get involved in the local church youth group than be a cheerleader for her school, offer to provide transportation to and from the youth group events if needed, arrange for carpools, and call the parents of existing or potential friends to get them to encourage their children to participate as well.

Modeling Your Own Friendship Choices

The second primary avenue through which you can exert an influence over the quality of your children's friendships is through the tried-and-true principle of modeling. Take a serious look at your own friends. Ask yourself what it is that has attracted you to them. How did you become friends in the first place? If you had it to do over again, would you still choose them as friends? If not, why not, and if so, why? If you wanted to make new friends who reflected the most important values that you wish to pass on to your children, where might you find them? How can you best use your own friends as models of normative ethical behavior for your children?

These are very important questions, yet most people seem to drift into their friendships by accident, rarely taking the time to think through exactly what it is they desire from their friends, and what they are willing to give in return. Adult friendships can have a powerful influence on helping to set the standards of behavior for your children. That is why I believe that you must look at every friendship, every adult in your life who will come in contact with your children, as if they are teachers whom you have selected to stand up in the front of your child's class and give a lecture or demonstration on "Why you should be just like me!"

In fact, that is very much what you are doing! Your friends serve as models for your children whether or not you want them to. As your children see you interacting with your friends, as they listen in to your conversations (which they always do at every opportunity), as they watch how you treat them and are treated in return, they are absorbing multiple lessons in social ethics according to the models that you have placed before them.

Examining Your Own Friendships

That is why it is so important to be conscious of the impact that your friendships have as models for your children. As parents begin to realize how important this really is, they sometimes find themselves disassociating themselves from the actions of their friends. They may realize (upon conscious scrutiny) that these friends have a habit of using racial slurs, or anti-Semitic expressions, or prejudicial language, and because of these decide that this is simply not the influence that they choose to have as part of their children's lives.

I have often heard parents tell me how embarrassed they had become over the realization that long-time friends were using expressions of speech that they now found offensive, and consequently didn't want their children emulating. Letting go of acquaintances of many years' duration is never a painless or easy task under any circumstances. But in the end, it might be important for you to recognize that allowing certain people to continue to be an important part of your life may result in the sending of mixed messages to your children regarding the behaviors and attitudes that you believe are appropriate to emulate.

Use your own friendships as a testing laboratory for the friendships of your children. Talk to your children about the kinds of friends that you have, why you have them as friends, the qualities you admire in them, the reasons why they remain a part of your life, the principle of give and take in a friendship, and the areas in which you give and receive in your own relationships. In this way, you are teaching your children that friendships are not to be taken lightly. You are teaching them something that they otherwise would simply never realize—that they ought to put at least as much thought and planning into choosing friends as they do into choosing what outfit they are going to wear just to be with those friends.

Teach Children to Take Friendships Seriously

Choosing friends is one of the most important choices that our children ever make. That is why one of the very best things that you can teach them is to take those friendships seriously. Tell your children that in many ways we are known by the friends that we keep. A great many people in our world will judge us solely according to the company we keep. They will pass judgment upon us and come to conclusions regarding our character, integrity, and personal qualities often solely upon the basis of whom we pick to be our friends.

Now no one would argue that such subjective personality and character judgments are "fair"; they aren't. But like it or not, that's the way real people make decisions about others in the real world in which we all live. Teach your children that there isn't much that anyone can do about the fact that other people pass judgment on us according to the company we keep, but at least we can have a say over the influences of others that we choose to bring into our lives.

Discussing Friendships

This is an extremely mature and sophisticated concept, and I urge parents to sit down and present it to their children in just that light. Tell them "I am going to talk to you about the impact of your friendships on the kind of person you become, and how others perceive you, even though I realize that it is a very adult, mature idea. I believe that you will understand it and that it is important for you to have a clear picture of how the world works when it comes to the role of friends in our lives. As an adult, I have the exact same experiences that you do when it comes to friends, and I try to be aware all the time of how my friendships affect my behavior and the kind of person that I am."

If you have chosen your own friends realizing that they are all ethical teachers and role models for your children, then it will be easier to point out the qualities in your friends that you admire, why you were attracted to them in the first place, and the social, emotional, and spiritual benefits that come through having these particular friendships.

That isn't to say that all friendships are to be based on self-conscious, carefully planned criteria and reasons—they aren't. Some people become our friends because we share certain common experiences (like serving on a jury, in the PTA, or at a volunteer organization), and some relationships we simply seem to fall into. Either way, as you approach the issue of teaching your children about the impact of friendships on their ethical action and development, it is an appropriate time to examine the friendships that you have, and see if they fit into an overall framework of ethical and moral behavior that you would be pleased for your children to recreate in their own lives.

The Right to Choose Our Friends

I truly believe that one of the greatest lessons you can teach your children is that they actually do have a lot of control over the friendships that they either nurture and embrace or reject. Too often our children are so insecure about themselves, and so desirous of praise, acceptance, and acknowledgment from their peers, that they will take on anyone as a friend simply because they are willing to have them as friends in return. By example, and by talking about your own experiences (both as a young person and an adult) in seeking out, creating and/or rejecting friendships, you can empower your children to do the same as well.

When your children hear that you are friends with others because there are qualities in them that you admire, when they realize that you have made conscious choices to be or not to be friends with others, it empowers them to see themselves in exactly the same light. This in turn helps them develop the internal, emotional strength to seek out those whose friendships they desire, and let go of those they don't. It allows them to feel that they have the power to make such choices, that consciously choosing the kinds of friends that fill their lives is both appropriate and praiseworthy. Perhaps even more importantly, it teaches them that they have an obligation to themselves to think about their friendships on a conscious level, and not simply "fall in" with whatever crowd happens to pass along.

Share Stories from Your Own Childhood

To make this happen you must play a crucial role. First, you must expect the same standards of yourself and your own friends that you demand from your children. Second, you have to be willing to share stories with your children of your own childhood friendships. Tell them about the ones that were nurturing, supportive, positive, and empowering, and tell them about the poor choices that you made as well. If there were friends in your past who took advantage of you and your naivete, tell your children about them. All children like to hear stories of their parents' childhoods, and it can be very liberating for your children to discover that you struggled with the exact same issues, the same insecurities, and the same desire to be popular that they may be struggling with now.

It is a wonderful experience for your children to learn lessons about themselves and about life from stories of your own past. True, they don't always result in the magic transformations that you often hope they might, but no matter what your intentions may be, you never really know exactly what impact such stories will have on your children. I remember one parent sharing with me how she told her daughter about the many times in junior high school that she ran home from school crying because the kids she wanted most to be friends with didn't seem interested in her. She told her how upset she got that the "popular" kids in school just didn't include her in their group in the way that she dreamed they would, and how deeply hurt she was all the time about it.

The woman was telling me this story, because she knew I was writing this book and wanted me to know that at the time of the telling it didn't seem to have any impact at all on her daughter. In fact, her daughter appeared to be rather bored and uninterested throughout the entire telling of the story. However, months later, when her daughter had experienced a particularly rough day at school with her friends, she suddenly repeated the story her mother had told her from her own childhood struggles with friends and said, "I guess if you lived through it then I can too. Anyway, those kids probably weren't worthy of your friendship in the first place if they couldn't see how terrific a person you were . . . and I don't suppose my so-called friends are either."

Your Stories Are Gifts from the Heart

The mother was amazed that her daughter had stored away the story in her memory banks to be recalled whenever her own ego was under attack by the insensitivities of fickle friends. She told me the story so that I might pass it on to you with a friendly reminder that "You just never know when something you tell your children gets through." Stories we share about ourselves with our children are like tiny, shiny pebbles on a sea shore. You never know when a passing child will scoop one up to be pulled out and admired with affection and delight some later rainy day.

She's right, of course, and that is exactly why it is important to share your stories, and open up to your children about these difficult and often traumatic emotional experiences of your own youth. In this way you help them to see you as a real person, who has experienced pains similar to their own. In fact, sharing your stories is one of the best ways I know to create bonds between you and your children, for it lets them know that you will probably be empathetic to their own struggles, because you have been through similar struggles of your own.

Be the Kind of Friend You Want Your Children to Have

Earlier I suggested that your challenge is to pick the kind of friends for yourself and to be the kind of friend that you would want your children both to become and to have. This is the key concept with friendships as it is in so many crucial areas of ethical development. "Mentor modeling," whether in your role as father or mother, sister or brother, employee or boss, parent, child, or friend is always the single most important way that you teach ethical behavior to your children.

When it comes to teaching them about how to be a friend to someone else, the best way they can learn is simply by watching and listening to you. How do you talk about your friends in front of your children? Is it with respect, caring, support, and encouragement? Or do you find yourself putting down your friends, expressing jealousy at a promotion, a new home, or a new car obtained by one of your friends? If your children acted exactly like you when it comes to their friends, would you be pleased with their behavior or want to change it? If you can say, "Yes, I would love my kids to act toward their friends the way that I act toward mine," then you are obviously on the right track.

Another important component to successfully modeling friendship skills is to make sure that you actually verbalize to your children the qualities in a friend that you admire, as well as those you try to express in your own behavior. This makes the entire process a conscious one, and allows them to understand that friendship is an area of life worth spending time thinking about and planning for the future. In that way the process of choosing and the experience of being a friend takes on a much more concrete, substantial place in their total understanding of the role of friendships in their lives.

What to Do About Television, or "Everyone Else Gets to Watch!"

What do you do about television? Statistics galore in books, magazines, and from television commentators themselves all proclaim the incredible amount of television that the average American youngster watches each week. For example, many claim that preschoolers watch an average of four hours per day. If that is true, it means that before they enter their first day of kindergarten they will have spent more time watching television than a student spends in four years of college classes!

The average elementary school child watches some 30 hours of television each week. By the time they graduate from high school, it is generally agreed that most kids will have spent some 15,000–18,000 hours watching television, compared to only 11,000 hours in the classroom. For many of us, this is a frightening revelation, since there is no doubt that all those thousands of hours of emotional, psychological, and social input from the television shows that bombard our children's senses have a profound effect on their self-image, understanding of their place within society, and expectations of what is appropriate behavior between individuals and groups within a community.

Television Does Have an Impact

Don't make the mistake of thinking for a moment that television has no impact on your children's moral education or the quality of the ethical decisions that they make as they grow into adolescence and young adulthood. The sheer amount of undesirable behavior, violence, cheap sexuality, abuse, corruption, addictions of all kinds, adultery, exploitation of the weak, murder, and rape take their inevitable toll on the expectations of behavior and concepts of the type of behavior necessary to achieve personal success that our children learn. By the age of twelve, the average American child will have viewed some 100,000 violent episodes on television and seen 13,000 people violently destroyed. Even cartoons, which we usually think of as "harmless" children's entertainment, now depict an average of twenty-six incidents of physical force with the intent to hurt or kill every hour.

It is simply foolish for us to pretend that such a barrage of violence is having no effect on the psyche of our children. It should be obvious from our own personal experiences of how we feel when we are walking out of the theater after seeing a movie with a lot of violence in it, that what our minds, both consciously and unconsciously, experience when we subject them to such violent images is a stimulation of our centers of aggressive behavior.

Exercising Control

So what is the appropriate response to all this violence that your children are subjected to by television? First, it's important to remember that you are in control of your child's television habits. You have the power and authority, and the responsibility to use it in order to direct and limit the television viewing of your child. "But all my friends are watching it," is not a compelling reason to allow your child to watch a show of which you disapprove.

Here are a few simple television suggestions:

1. Remember that there are alternatives to television. Encourage your children to read books, and take the time to read to them. It is a wonderful, positive, emotionally nurturing bonding opportunity for you and your children. Teaching them the value of reading, introducing them to literature, and in the process demonstrating to them how important they are to you by giving to them of your most valuable possession—your time—all make encouraging reading by and participating in reading with your children the most valuable and positive alternative to television.

2. Set limits for each day and week on the amount of time they may watch television.

3. Don't put a television in your child's bedroom. Or, if you do, set it up so that there is a lock on it (you can buy them commercially), and use it to limit their television time.

4. Read the television guide. Watch the shows your child likes to watch, so that you can determine the content. Only after you have seen one or two episodes of a show will you be in a position to make informed and intelligent decisions about which shows you want your child to spend time watching.

5. Watch shows together and discuss them in a kind of "family time" afterward. Television can be a highly educational medium, and it can be made to serve your ethical parenting needs. Discuss the decisions that people made in the show, how your children

might have decided, the choices you would have made, and the implications of those choices.

6. Encourage a host of other non-television activities for your children to do alone, with friends, or with you. They can play active games or sports outside or board games inside, play music, read, exercise, build something, paint, draw, write a letter, call a relative, cook or bake something as a family, make up stories (then write them down to share again later), visit a museum or gallery, invite a friend to play, do their homework, or find a hundred other alternatives every single day to sitting like a lump and staring at the television screen.

7. Create weekly family activities to do with your children. These can include things like going to the zoo, visiting a children's museum, going to art galleries, visiting a theme park, going on a picnic, taking a trip to the beach, swimming in a friend's backyard pool (or your own if you have one), playing sports together, taking a hike in a park, creating a family home building project, creating a family art project, volunteering as a family to visit senior citizens in a convalescent home, bringing food to a homeless shelter, tutoring reading to someone who can't read (millions of all ages and races are illiterate in America), picking a political candidate to work for, passing out petitions for a project or cause that your family endorses, creating board games to play, visiting a planetarium or a science museum, or any other of hundreds of family activities that will bring you closer together and reinforce the positive, relationship-building and life-affirming values that you desire to instill in your children.

When All Is Said and Done . . .

In the end, it's helpful to keep in mind that regardless of the activities you create to share with your children, their choice of friendships, the decisions they make regarding whom to choose as their peers, and even the role models that they will choose to emulate, ultimately will be of their choosing, and not your own. You can give them guidance, you can give them direction, you can show them through your own behavior by modeling the kinds of friends that you choose to have in your own life in the hopes that they will emulate your choices as well, but beyond that the choices will always be theirs.

The thought I want to leave you with on this subject is that despite the apparent lack of control that you can exert over your children's friendship choices, and in spite of all the anxieties and quiet fears that every parent harbors over the potential negative influence that unknown peers may exert over their children, ultimately after you have done the best you can, the only thing left to do, is trust your children. Trust that when all is said and done, your children will usually make the right decisions. Trust that the values and ethics that you have instilled in them through the words that you teach and the examples that you live will have sufficient impact on the core of their being to counteract whatever transitory effect the friendship-of-the-month might have.

Give Your Children Freedom

Though there will certainly be periods in your children's lives when the esteem of their peers will weigh in much more heavily than your own, underneath it all will still solidly be resting, the foundation of their sense of right and wrong that they have learned from you. All you need do is pause for a moment to consider your own need or desire for parental approval, no matter how old you might be, to realize that such desires really never go away. Even after our parents are dead, there is still such a powerful emotional tie that many of us respond to life in part based on whether or not our actions would still meet with our parents' approval.

Obviously it is important to pay attention to the kinds of friends that your children choose, and if necessary to do what you can to protect your children from self-destructive behavior. However, beyond protecting them from getting physically hurt by their choices, remember that part of the inevitable process of growth and maturation that all of us must pass through involves often painful lessons in the ebb and flow of peer approval and disapproval. Give your children the freedom to discover those lessons for themselves, always knowing that you will be there to lend a sympathetic ear, to hold their hand when necessary, to catch their tears when inevitable, and to give them your unconditional love and support.

In the next chapter, we will look at what I consider to be the ultimate, bottom-line responsibility that parents have toward their children, without which there is little hope of raising the kind of human beings who will help transform our world into all that it has the potential to become.

Nine

Teaching Your Child That Life Has Meaning

Life without commitment isn't worth living.
Malcolm Fishwick

We have finally arrived at what I believe to be the most important challenge of all. For after all the discipline techniques have been taught and the intricacies of moral development have been mastered; after the roots of our Judeo–Christian ethics have been shared and your children have been raised with a strong sense of positive self-esteem; when all is said and done, perhaps your greatest parenting challenge is to inspire your children with the faith that there is ultimate meaning to life.

Most of the time it seems as though we merely live our lives going from day to day, caught up in the hustle and bustle of our everyday existence, focusing on the narrow vision of little more than the immediate moment. We go to school or we work to support ourselves and our families; we raise our kids or get lost in the complex ins and outs of trying to create a successful loving relationship with another human being. Through it all we so easily lose sight of the higher purposes for which we were created, the loftier visions to which we can aspire. Communicating that vision, grasping hold with both hands to the certainty that there are higher purposes to life, then passing that conviction on lovingly to the next generation is possibly the single most important job we will ever have in our lifetime.

I believe that our job as parents is to communicate to our children not only the possibility that life has meaning, but the reality that it is they who have the responsibility to bring that meaning into being in their daily lives. Our job is to inspire our children to see the world as filled with opportunities for greatness, for beauty, for joy, for blessings beyond measure including the transforming, life-changing power of love.

On the most basic and functional level, life has meaning, if we live it as if it does. In one sense, it's as simple as that. If our children will live their lives as if they can bring meaning and purpose into the world each day, then that's exactly what will happen—they will discover their own meaning and purpose just in the process of life itself.

The reason I can speak so confidently about your children's ability to create a sense of purpose and meaning in their lives is because, in all humility, I believe that I know the secret to discovering that meaning. It's a secret, not of my own invention, but that has been part of many spiritual traditions for thousands of years. It has served as the primary key to fulfillment, joy, happiness, and satisfaction from generation to generation and from culture to culture throughout the world.

As You Think, So Shall You Become

This simple formula for success can be found not only in sacred religious writings, but in contemporary motivational literature, corporate management seminars, and in books, magazines, and tapes that have flooded the market in recent years, designed to inspire every individual to maximize his or her potential. In its most direct form, this secret can be expressed through the following simple maxim: *as you think, so shall you become.*

"As you think, so shall you become," has been the key to success for literally thousands of years, for men and women in all walks of life, from every culture in the world. It lies beneath the successes of every inventor who ever dreamed of bringing into existence something never before seen by human beings; it lies behind the successes of every political leader who ever inspired the men and women of his or her country to do great deeds and accomplish great miracles.

Everything that has ever been created by any human being in history began as an idea in the mind of a single individual. Everything we see around us—every invention, item of convenience, book, television set, radio, automobile, airplane, cup, plate, fork, spoon, broom, shirt, or pair of shoes—began in the vision of one person's mind, long before it could be brought into the reality of being.

Possibility Thinking

This is why teaching your children to approach all life with the attitude that life is filled with endless possibilities is so important. It is a necessary ingredient to encourage acts of creative thinking, to empowering them along the life-long path of emotional or spiritual growth and development, and to opening up their minds to the multitude of possibilities for transforming the quality of the world around them.

Someone once said "What the mind can conceive and believe, the mind can achieve." So, too, with the minds of your own children. Part of the challenge of parenting is to fill your children's minds so full of the excitement at the possibilities that life has to offer, that they conceive of a world that nurtures, supports, and sustains everyone, and then do their part to make it a reality.

We Are Like Pebbles in a Pond

You have the responsibility to teach your children that the quality of the world in which they live will be directly proportional to the quality of their own behavior within that world. In a real sense, no one really lives in "the world," per se, anyway. Instead, we actually live within tiny circles of relationships and interactions with friends, family, acquaintances, colleagues, co-workers, and strangers. It is within this small circle of relationships that our behavior has the greatest impact. But since all life can be seen as the interaction of the small circles of individuals projected into the general society, by concentrating on exhibiting the kind of behavior that we believe will most likely create a life of positive value and meaning for us, like a pebble in the pond our actions will automatically send ripples influencing the lives of others around us.

The Power of Attitude

This is why the second key to empowering your children is this: they need to learn that not only do they get to choose the behavior that determines the quality of their lives, they get to choose how they react to the circumstances of life that they didn't choose. This is due to the fact that when it comes to making life meaningful, or feeling fulfilled, satisfied, and competent to take control of their lives, the single most important word in the English language is *attitude*. Without question, it isn't the circumstances of life that determine how they feel about themselves or the world in which they live each day, it is their attitude. Attitude can transform frustration into excitement, disappointment into anticipation, failure into success.

You may remember the famous story of how Thomas Edison was approached by a reporter on the day in which his one thousandth attempt to create an electric light bulb failed. The reporter asked, "Mr. Edison, how does it feel to fail so many times?" Edison replied with surprise, "Fail? I haven't failed at all. I now know one thousand ways *not* to make an electric light bulb."

You see, it was Edison's remarkable, consistent positive attitude about life and his deep conviction that ultimately he would succeed at whatever he set out to do that was primarily responsible for his phenomenal record of success. Your children could do a lot worse for sure, than modeling their attitudes about life after that of Thomas Edison. After all, Edison is credited with creating more inventions and holding more patents than any other human being in history!

That is why as a parent, your job is to pass on that same optimism, that same attitude of positive self-expectation that continually inspired Edison to envision great things, and along the way transformed the lives of millions throughout the world. No, it doesn't matter if your child becomes a famous inventor, doctor, scientist, railroad conductor, athlete, musician, mechanic, tree-trimmer, teacher, or nurse. What *does* matter is that they develop a sufficiently positive attitude about themselves and life that they will constantly hear the quiet whisper within the inner recesses of their minds, "Whatever happens in your life, you can transform it into something positive." This is the famous "When life gives you lemons, make lemonade" philosophy, which has been the mainstay and inspiration of creative, successful people since the beginning of time.

Indeed, it is primarily their attitude about life, that will determine whether they experience life itself as positive or negative, a success or failure, and not the circumstances themselves. The most dramatic example of this can be found in the work of the world renowned psychiatrist Dr. Viktor Frankl.

Goals, Dreams, and Visions
Can Sustain Life Itself

Dr. Frankl had the misfortune of being interned in the Auschwitz death camp during World War II. While there, he watched as thousands of prisoners died under the most dehumanizing and brutal of circumstances. As a psychiatrist he was fascinated with the questions of why some lived and others died, given the fact that their circumstances seemed on the surface to be so similar. Thus, when he was liberated from the concentration camp, he decided to dedicate the rest of his life to the pursuit of that knowledge.

The results of his study can be read in his profoundly moving book *Man's Search for Meaning*. In it, Frankl shares his discovery of the single most important factor in determining which prisoners survived and which perished. He teaches us that the power of the individual's will to live is actually grounded in a conviction that there is some thing, some idea, some goal, some dream, some vision greater than the self that is worth living for. He discovered that it was primarily this sense of needing to live so that they could accomplish some personal mission that separated one group from the other.

In some cases, the goal was to be reunited with a loved one. In others it was to fulfill a life-long dream, professional goal, or even simply to get revenge for the inhumanity of their brutal and dehumanizing treatment at the hands of the Nazis. In all cases, however, the key lay in this driving internal sense of having a greater purpose, a transcending goal that kept them going against all odds.

It's Not the Circumstances

The reason I share with you Viktor Frankl's work in the context of a book on raising ethical children is to point out that the essential principle is the same, whether life itself is at stake, or the goal is simply to lead the successful and fulfilled life which is every parent's dream for their children. What Frankl realized is that it wasn't the circumstances of being in the concentration camp that made the difference, since all prisoners were suffering from the same external experiences. What truly made the difference, even in this most extreme, degrading situation with its apparent total powerlessness was, above all else, the *attitude* of the prisoners.

That same principle can guide the lives of your children as well. No matter what happens to them in life, no matter what circumstances they might find themselves thrust into, it will ultimately be their attitude that will determine the impact of those circumstances on their lives. What makes this idea so powerful is that it places both the responsibility and the control over the quality of your children's lives primarily in their hands. That is why I believe that one of the most lasting gifts that you can give your children is this gift of possibility thinking, this positive mental attitude toward all of life.

The Attitude of Hope

As a rabbi who has worked with and counseled families of all kinds for some twenty years, I know of the incredible litany of tragedies, traumas, sickness, death, injury, frustration, and failures that can invade a family's life. Time and again I have watched as hopes have been dashed in a moment of recklessness, lives crushed by drunk drivers, careers destroyed by seemingly capricious external forces.

Yet in spite of the tragedies that at first appear so overwhelming, I have also had the privilege of witnessing the remarkable, miraculous recovery of family relationships, the healing of lives, the turning around of these tragedies into triumphs, the transformation from despair to commitment to success. I believe deeply that none of those miraculous turnarounds could have taken place without an attitude of hope and of faith in the future and in the individual's ability to change, to grow, and to make a difference in their own and other's lives.

The Gift That Keeps on Giving

It has been this positive mental attitude about life more than any other single quality that I believe is responsible for the sense of fulfillment and satisfaction of almost every successful person I have ever met. This is truly a gift that keeps on giving. I guarantee that as a parent, no matter how hard you might try, you cannot protect your child from the slings and arrows of life. You can never be there every minute to watch and protect. You can't hold their hand every time they cross the street, take their tests for them, drive their cars, pick their relationships, choose their romances, or control their diets.

In a sense, to be a parent is to be forever in the process of letting go. It is a life-long experience of holding your breath and praying that everything will be OK—that you will get the phone call that says they arrived safely; that you will meet their friends and be relieved about the people they have chosen to spend their time with; that you will stand next to them at their wedding and know that their spouse-to-be will be a loving, supportive, nurturing co-partner for life.

But if you are honest, you will accept the reality that all these are pretty much out of your control. What is in your control, however, is to make sure that during these crucial parenting years you do everything within your power to give your children the positive expectation that they can affect the quality of their own lives. You can teach them that even when what happens around them seems to be out of their control, how they *react* to what happens is *always* in their control.

When all is said and done, how your children react is actually more important than whatever it is that's causing them to react in the first place. Events come and go, and the experiences of life are transitory, disappearing in a moment. What lasts is the attitude that your children bring to each moment, the interpretation of each event that they take away with them. In contemporary political language, it is the "spin" that your children give to each and every passing event which determines whether those events will have a positive or negative impact on their lives; it is never really the events themselves.

Transcending Powerlessness

I am spending so much time on this issue because although it is such a simple concept, it is one of the most profound lessons that you could ever teach your children. One of the worst things in life is to feel powerless. Next to feeling invisible, unacknowledged, and therefore worthless as a human being, the feeling of being out of control and unable to determine whether or not your life is successful is among the most devastating and debilitating of all feelings. When you give your children the gift of a positive mental attitude, you are giving them the tools to transcend the apparent powerlessness of life.

Of course, one of the important ways in which you help your children along the path of developing this positive mental attitude is by demonstrating that they are respected, accepted, and appreciated for their internal worth, and not merely for external accomplishments. Children enjoy being responsible. Children enjoy feeling competent. Children are enthusiastic about being able to help others, and this feeling of competence must begin its development based upon how they are treated at home.

Give them tasks to perform that they can do well, and in turn they will feel good about themselves. Assign them responsibilities around your home that will continually build up their sense of accomplishment, competence, and self-worth, and you will be doing more for them than teaching all the math, science, and history in the world.

Raising ethical children is the result of the accumulation of those small moments of building self-esteem, coupled with the lessons learned by observing you and how you interact with family, friends, colleagues, and even enemies. It is the result of taking one step at a time, teaching one lesson at a time, giving one example at a time of acting ethically, talking ethically, and measuring others by the same standards.

Measuring Your Children by Moral Standards

Your children need to know by what you say and how you act, that you measure the value and worth of others by the strength of their character, and not by the amount of their bank account, the size of their house, or the make of their car. The importance of this lesson can hardly be overstressed, since they will naturally assume that you will measure their worth and value according to the same general standards you apply to others.

In other words, if you judge others by their material success, your children will see material success as the primary indicator of their own value as human beings as well. Knowing this can help you prevent inadvertently sending the wrong messages to your children, because it forewarns you about the need to consistently demonstrate where your real values lie.

The key is to figure out how to link the fact that what you most admire in others is their character and moral, ethical, and spiritual values to your expectations and relationship with your own children. Judge them by the same standards as you judge others. Reward them for acts of morality, acts of caring, acts of compassion toward others, examples of ethical decision making that you admire, and not for the "accomplishments" that merely lead to the accumulation of things.

Redefining Rewardable Behavior

A good example of how parents too often focus on external accomplishments without even noticing involves the issue of grades in school. Often grades become merely a commodity to be prized for their rate of exchange, traded for dollars, privileges, favors, and the like. Not all authorities agree with me, but I believe that paying children for getting good grades actually devalues the experience. It teaches children that all life is a giant barter game, first with grades and later with their work, time, muscle, or creativity. It takes the grade out of the realm of a personal triumph or accomplishment, and instead reduces it to an object of the marketplace.

I would prefer that my child feel good about accomplishments for their own sake. I want her to know that the grades are merely symbols of her previous dedication and study. I'd rather reward her for having the integrity to follow through with a specific commitment that she might make to me, her teacher, or herself about the quality of her work at school, than be fixated on rewarding her purely according to the grade she might get in the class. I want the reward to focus on the qualities of character that the grades symbolize, not the grades themselves.

The Importance of Keeping Commitments

I would be happier rewarding my child for keeping her agreement to do a specific amount of work, study a specific number of hours each week, or write a specific number of papers each semester, than for the grade that she might get as a result of that work. In this way I am reinforcing that my own particular values dictate that her integrity is more important than her grades; her ability to follow through with commitments, her ability to exercise good judgment, the strength of character she demonstrates by staying home to study or write the paper instead of going with friends to the movie, *these* are the qualities I admire, these are what I consider worthy of rewards.

Our Value Lies in the Contribution We Make

The goal of ethical parenting is to raise children who experience their personal worth and value as directly related to contributions they make to others and not in terms of the number of things they collect. "It is better to give than to receive" is a famous cliché because it contains a fundamental truth about the nature of the universe. Most people make the mistake of thinking that this aphorism is simply talking about the difference between "getting" and "giving." Most see it as teaching a kind of mild altruism, whereby one "should" feel happier giving gifts than receiving them.

What it really teaches is that fundamental self-worth is not a function of what we get, but of how we see ourselves in relation to others. And how we see ourselves is ultimately related to whether we are a "giver" or a "taker" in life. The givers are those whose approach to others is "How can I make a difference in your life, what can I add to it, how can I make it better?" There are fewer feelings better in life than that of knowing that you have done something to touch the life of another person. It is *this* sense of "giving" that the famous aphorism refers to, not the giving of physical, material presents.

The takers in life are those who see life from the perspective of need, want, and scarcity. They imagine the world as children might regard a small box of candy being passed around a large and bustling living room. The children know that if they don't act quickly, assertively, and in their own self-interest, by the time the box gets around the room, there will probably not be any candy left.

Love Is in Limitless Supply

Life, for many, is a game of "grab the candy box before all the candy is given away." If most people were able to see life as being primarily about love and not about things, they would have a lot less anxiety and a lot less fear of loss. After all, unlike a box of candy (which interestingly enough often serves as a physical symbol of love), love comes in a limitless supply.

Actually, the candy box is a good analogy, since too often both adults and children mistake the external, physical symbol of love for the love itself. When that happens, it is easy to feel that when the symbols are gone, so is the love. This is one of the reasons why you find some people aggressively pursuing those external symbols—it is to ensure that they don't lose all the love that they so desperately crave, and which the symbols represent.

Others recognize that the symbols (like the box of candy, money for grades, new bike, car, house . . .) are only external things, while the love itself comes from a much deeper and more profound place with no boundaries, no end, no barriers. Part of raising ethical children involves creating the kind of family life whereby your children learn firsthand, directly by example, the difference between real love and love's symbols.

It is best not to use gifts, toys, money, privileges, or things as a reward for being the right kind of person. Here ancient Jewish tradition is wise when it counsels, "The reward for doing the right thing, is doing the right thing." That is, we want our children to discover how good it feels to do the right thing for its own sake, because it is the right thing to do, and not simply because they may get something physical as a result.

The Meaning of Life
Is in the Loving

Ultimately all authority as a parent must be based on love. Without love as the foundation of your relationship, love that is demonstrated in innumerable ways to your children each day, you will never truly establish and maintain an authentic foundation of authority with them.

As we have already seen (in Chapter 5), two of the key elements of your parental behavior that communicate to your children your love are *time* and *focus*. When anyone sees that you are willing to give your most valuable possession, your time to them, it can't help but make them feel important, significant, and valuable in your sight.

Time is a rare and limited commodity that comes around only once, and when it passes never returns. Each day has a finite number of hours in it, each year is precious, each moment is a gift, so when we give some of that valuable time to another human being, whether a friend, colleague, spouse, or child, we are giving something that we will never get back. That is why we feel so good when people give us their undivided attention, and that is why simply making yourself available to listen is such an important and crucial parenting tool.

Every child has painful or upsetting experiences at school or while playing with friends. Every child comes home from time to time in need of a hug, whether physical or emotional. Listening to them, giving them your full one-on-one attention, is the simplest way of letting them know that you are on their side. Often there is nothing you can really do to ease their pain or make the problem go away. You can't fight all your children's battles, and you can't ride in on a white charger to slay the dragons on the playground every day. But what you can do is to give your children emotional support and the strong foundation that your love can provide to help them discover their own inner strength to face the sometimes difficult experiences of childhood relationships.

They need to know that you are behind them. They need to know that you will always care. They need to know that you will be there for them in any way you can whenever they need you. This knowledge, this certainty of parental support, is an essential element of raising children who are emotionally secure, who are confident of their ability to face life's ups and downs, and who will be able to recognize that there is ultimate meaning to life in spite of its temporary pains and disappointments. With children, time translates into feeling valued, cared for, loved, and lovable.

The same goes for the issue of focus. Focus communicates that your child is important enough to you to give not only your time, but your attention. It communicates the crucial emotional message that they are noticed; that they exist; that they are worth your attention, your time, and your focus.

Intentions Count

Very often parents succeed in spite of themselves and their particular parenting choices. This is usually because the emotional message remains constant. Children literally feel that their parents love and support them and truly want what's best for them, in spite of parental inconsistencies of behavior, confused rules, and inadequately monitored consequences.

This underlying message of fundamental love is communicated in 1,000 different ways and has the remarkable ability most of the time of compensating for occasional outbursts, frustrations, and actions you might otherwise regret. That's why I urge you with all my heart not to be too hard on yourself. Have faith that the love that you feel and the desire that you have for your children to grow up healthy, well-adjusted, with positive self-esteem and confidence will ultimately be communicated on the levels that really count.

An Environment of Love = An Environment of Meaning

Although there are no magic keys to unlocking the secret door of self-esteem, feelings of self-worth, and love in your children, there are several practical everyday techniques that will go a long way toward creating the kind of caring, supportive, loving environment in your home that will create in its wake a sense that life itself has meaning and purpose.

Active Encouragement

An important practical technique for nurturing a loving ethical home environment is called *active encouragement*. Active encouragement means helping your child to pursue those activities, relationships, and involvements that will help build confidence and a sense of accomplishment in life.

Every child has areas of strengths and weaknesses. Every child is drawn more to some activities and experiences than others. Some gravitate to music, others to art, others to math and science, others to computers. Some children find great satisfaction in athletics, others in karate, others in making jewelry or cooking, still others in competing in the local frisbee-throwing tournament.

Successful parents are those who learn to encourage their children to pursue the activities that they enjoy, even if the parent doesn't! Too many parents push their kids into trying out for baseball or soccer teams, taking endless ballet lessons, or spending excruciating hours on end in front of a piano because the parents decide that their children "should" participate in these activities for their own good.

Most often this is a surefire prescription for disaster and resentment. Often many, many years go by before individuals will even consider trying any activity they were forced to endure as children. What you want to do as a parent is to help your children discover what they do like, not force them to do what they don't like. Encouraging participation in pleasurable activities is one of the best ways I know to ensure that your children will feel good about themselves, and therefore about life itself. Since all of us enjoy doing things that we are good at, encouraging your children to participate in activities that they like is inevitably a self-validating, self-confidence-building experience.

Set Clear Limits

A second practical technique is to *set clear limits* on your children's behavior. It sounds much easier than it is. Nearly every parent I know at one time or another has fallen victim to the parental sin of "I'm willing to do just about anything to get this child off my back." In too many families, kids learn that if they cry, whine, beg, cajole, ask incessantly, badger, make the right face, or just persist long enough they will eventually get what they want.

Parents begin by giving in to candy or cookies as a form of child pacification when children are younger, and end up handing over the car keys to get them out of their hair when they get older. Setting clear limits on your children's behavior isn't always easy, but it is always important. Of course, all of us slip now and then. All of us give in from time to time and often regret it later. But if you can set limits that are reasonable and appropriate to the kind of moral values that you wish to teach your children, and keep to them most of the time, you will be giving them another important parenting gift.

Children need limits. Part of their job in life as they grow is to constantly test the limits that parents, teachers, and society place in front of them. This is part of the important process of individual identity formation, of allowing them to work out on their own those values that they will embrace and those that they will ultimately reject (regardless of even your best efforts).

At such moments, what your children really want and need is for you to put your foot down. What they want and need is for you to stand up for your principles, to insist that they follow the ethical standards and guidelines that you have articulated in the past, and they want you to pull in the reins of freedom to conform with these guidelines. This is one of the most important tools you have as a parent for letting your children know that you really do have ethical expectations and that you believe in what you teach. You "walk your talk" and therefore can be trusted that your "yes" is a yes, and your "no" is a no.

An important extension of this same general technique is that your children must see you apply similar standards to your own behavior that you apply to theirs. When you demonstrate through your actions mutual respect for their feelings, concerns, dreams, and plans, you communicate once again that your values are part of a total life context within which they can safely learn, grow, and struggle with their evolving individual identity.

Something as simple as saying "please" or "thank you" to your children communicates that you see them as human beings of individual worth and value, regardless of their particular age. It models for them the kind of behavior you expect from them, and allows you to demand that they live up to the standards you yourself express in your everyday life. When parents act in accordance with the same standards of manners that they expect from their children, children learn the importance of mutual respect and of acting in a way that allows them to get along with others in a mutually validating way.

Verbal Self-Control

A third crucial technique is to exercise *verbal self-control.* Whoever came up with the childhood taunt "Sticks and stones may break my bones but words will never harm me" must have been comatose through their entire childhood! Broken bones usually mend in a few weeks or months, but crushed egos, shattered self-images that are broken by words spoken in anger, sarcastic put downs, or verbal belittling may never be whole again. Every one of us can remember words spoken by parents or teachers, even 30, 40, or 50 years later, that crushed us emotionally; undermined our sense of self-esteem; and made us feel foolish, worthless, or stupid.

The Power of Parental Approval

Frankly, words are the single most powerful weapons in our personal arsenal. They can build up or tear down—make us feel like a million dollars, or the most useless human beings on earth. All too often parents are practically oblivious to the incredible power that they possess through the words that they speak to their children. After all, parents are not only their children's primary caregivers, they are the ultimate authority for everything in life. Up to a certain age, before children begin the process of individuation and begin in earnest separating themselves from their parents emotionally, being a parent has almost godlike qualities—whatever you say is the truth about life.

That is why parents can destroy our fragile egos so easily. As children we rely upon our parents for our sense of self, to signal whether or not we are valuable and acceptable as human beings. In fact, many psychologists argue that parental approval is the single most important goal of a child's life. If that is true, imagine the powerful impact that your words have on your child's developing ego, and imagine how important it is whether they are words of praise or ridicule to the healthy identity formation of your child.

This is why verbal self-control is such an important technique to practice. Yes, of course it's easy to let yourself get carried away from time to time in the heat of an angry moment. All of us have been guilty of slipping now and then. Besides, I don't believe that it's the occasional moment of anger or emotional heat that destroys our children's self-esteem. In fact, there are times when disapproval spoken in the passion of the moment communicates to our children our love for them, our deep concern for their well-being and just how important they really are to us.

Avoiding Abusive Patterns

What really destroys a child's sense of self-worth and ability to see meaning and purpose in life is a pattern of consistent disinterest and verbal abuse. Just as perhaps the single most devastating form of punishment you can inflict upon children is to ignore them or place them in isolation, so too, any consistent verbal abuse that communicates to children that their parents really don't care about them or love them is the the most destructive behavior in which parents can engage.

Verbal self-control means setting standards and limits to your own behavior as much as the behavior of your children. It means making conscious decisions in advance as a parent, and if you are co-parenting, deciding with your partner as part of a team, exactly what kind of messages you want to communicate to your children through the words you speak. After you have first made this determination, it is then easier to identify the specific words you do want to say, and phrases you want to emphasize in moments when you are reprimanding or disciplining your children.

Setting Verbal Communication Goals

A very useful technique that I often recommend to parents is that they sit together (or as a single parent you can do it by yourself) with a blank notepad and write at the top "VERBAL COMMUNICATION GOALS." Then on the left side of the page, write down the goals for your children regarding their sense of self-worth; their sense of social responsibility; and their behavior interacting with peers, authority figures, or other adults that you wish to achieve as the outcome of your parenting decisions.

After you have completed this initial list, on the right side of the same page (or pages) begin to list the specific language that you believe will, if consistently spoken, help your children to achieve your behavior and self-esteem goals. After you have listed the words and phrases that you believe if used will lead them toward your agreed-upon goals, at the end of the page make another heading called "WORDS TO AVOID."

Under "WORDS TO AVOID" list all the negative words, put-downs, belittling phrases, humiliating expressions, and insulting terminology that you want to avoid using with your children. No one is perfect, and all of us make mistakes, most of us more often than we would like. Having a handy list of words to use and words to avoid using with your children can be a very helpful tool in your daily desire to reinforce the best both within yourself and your children. It gives you a reference point, something to refer to from time to time as a constant reminder. Some parents I know read through their list at least once every day, just to keep the positive phrases fresh in their minds and remind themselves of what they want to avoid.

Be the Adult That They Can Grow Up to Be

Once again you may have noticed, that in demonstrating what I mean by the importance of teaching your children the value of character over accumulation, I have shared an example of something that is best taught by personal example. By now I'm sure you have realized that the power of personal example is, without question, the running theme of this book. In fact, if I were to write the entire book in one sentence (of course then no one would buy it), I would simply write, *be the kind of person that you want your children to become.* I truly believe that if every one followed that small but powerful bit of advice, this book and others like it would be entirely superfluous.

One of the greatest and most demanding challenges is to measure yourself by the standards with which you measure your children. Hold up the same yardstick for ethical behavior, character, and personal worth to yourself that you would apply to your children and others in judging the quality of their character. If you are not able to feel good about yourself as a result of how you treat others and the contributions that you make to improving the quality of life in your community (through your family, participation in civic organizations, churches, synagogues, and other groups) then how can you expect your children to do the same? This, too must be taught by example.

If your children hear you sitting at the dinner table expressing frustration, anger, jealousy, and unhappiness with your life because of the car you can't drive, the house you can't live in, or the things you can't buy, no amount of words or lofty sentiments from you, their teachers, or the local minister's sermon will most likely convince them that self-worth is measured by any standards other than material.

Of course being a parent isn't easy under any circumstances. But being a parent when times are tough financially, when you are falling short of your material goals, or are frustrated in your career is even harder. Add to that the desire to inspire your children to be ethical, caring, loving, responsible human beings, and without question parenting becomes one of the greatest challenges on the planet.

The Courage to Care

It takes great courage and profound faith to undertake the task of raising ethical children. To do so even recognizing all the myriad forces of the world that seem to conspire against you, even while realizing how much is out of your hands and beyond your control is truly an act of the deepest love for your children. It would be much easier to throw up your hands in despair, give in to the influences of materialism, consumerism, and instant self-gratification that are all around you. So, when in spite of all this you persist in reading books like this one, learning from the successes and frustrations of others, doing your best to pass on a legacy of values, ethics, morality, and goodness to your child, you ought to feel proud of your commitment and dedication.

The very fact that you care enough about raising ethical children, that you take the time to develop an awareness of the skills, behaviors, and attitudes necessary to inspire and empower your children to be the very best that they can be is a tribute to your faith in yourself, in your children, and the future of our society. Every time you teach them both by your words and your actions what it is to be an ethical human being, you are beating back the hounds of helplessness and boldly declaring that the kind of person you are actually does make a difference. And that lesson is important enough to be taught by you and your children over and over and over again until it is believed by every child on our planet.

Know That You're Imperfect, and Have Faith That You'll Succeed

Have the courage to be imperfect. Have the courage to make mistakes. Have the courage to admit when those mistakes are made, and the courage to include your children in the important decisions of their lives. Have the courage to believe that with all your faults, false-starts, mistakes, and errors of judgment, your children will still love you. And have faith that through it all, they will grow up to be healthy, productive, competent, caring, ethical human beings.

Your never-ending task is to let them know how much you love them, how important and valuable you think they are as human beings, how much faith you have in their own abilities to make intelligent and appropriate decisions, and how certain you are that they will grow up to be the kind of person who demonstrates true caring for others.

As we have seen throughout these nine chapters, there are no magic answers, no money-back guarantees, no unassailable techniques that will ensure that any of us will be successful in raising ethical, empathetic, well-adjusted, fulfilled children. Yet even without the absolutes, I believe so profoundly not only that life has ultimate meaning and purpose that you can discover together with your children, but that they can be empowered to recognize their own ability to make a difference in the world around them.

I have tried to share as many ideas, theoretical concepts, and practical hands-on techniques for inspiring your children to discover that meaning in life as I could. I also know for certain that if every parent in our world were as dedicated to raising ethical, compassionate, moral children as you are, then the world would become all that we know it can be. Have faith in yourself. Have the courage to take the bold steps, to set the limits, to activate the consequences, to fill your children's cup of self-esteem to the very top, and most of all, to live your life each day so that you would be proud if your children followed in your footsteps. Then every day will be a cause for celebration, and the world our children will create together will be a world of love, a world of moral vision, and a world of peace.

Bibliography

Bettelheim, Bruno. *A Good Enough Parent*. New York: Vintage Books, 1988.

Brenner, Barbara. *Love and Discipline*. New York: Ballantine Books, 1983.

Church, Joseph, and Stone, Joseph, L. *Childhood and Adolescence: A Psychology of the Growing Person*. New York: Random House, 1979.

Clemes, H. and Bean, R. *Self-Esteem: The Key to Your Child's Well-Being*. New York: G. P. Putnam's Sons, 1981.

Coles, Robert. *The Moral Life of Children*. Boston: Houghton Mifflin Company, 1986.

Coopersmith, Stanley. *The Antecedents of Self-Esteem*. San Francisco: W. H. Freeman, 1967.

Curry, Nancy E., and Johnson, Carl N. *Beyond Self-Esteem: Developing a Genuine Sense of Human Value*. Washington, D.C.: National Association for the Education of Young Children, 1990.

Dinkmeyer, Don. "Teaching Responsibility, Developing Personal Accountability Through Natural and Logical Consequences." In *Experts Advise Parents*, edited by Eileen Shiff. New York: Delta Books, 1987, p. 183.

Dinkmeyer, Don, and McKay, Gary D. *Raising a Responsible Child*. New York: Fireside Books, 1973.

Dreikurs, R., and Grey, L. *A New Approach to Discipline: Logical Consequences*. New York: Hawthorne Books, 1968.

Dyer, Wayne W. *What Do You Really Want for Your Children?* New York: Avon Books, 1985.

Eimers, Robert, and Aitchison, Robert. *Effective Parents, Responsible Children.* New York: McGraw-Hill, 1977.

Fitzpatrick, Jean Grasso. *Something More.* New York: Viking Penguin, 1991.

Foster, Constance J. *Developing Responsibility in Children.* Chicago: Senior Research Associates, 1953.

Ginott, Haim G. *Between Parent and Child.* New York: Macmillan, 1965.

Glenn, Stephen H., and Nelson, Jane. *Raising Self-Reliant Children in a Self-Indulgent World.* Rocklin, Calif.: Prima Publishing, 1989.

Grusec, Joan E., and Arnason, Lynn. "Consideration for Others: Approaches to Enhancing Altruism." In *The Young Child: Reviews of Research,* vol. 3, edited by Shirley G. Moore and Catherine R. Cooper. Washington, D.C.: National Association for the Education of Young Children, 1982, pp. 159–174.

Harris, James M. *You and Your Child's Self-Esteem.* New York: Warner Books, 1989.

Hendricks, Dr. Howard. "Family Happiness Is Homemade," *Family Concern,* vol. 13, no. 3 (March 1989).

Kohlberg, Lawrence. "Development of Moral Character and Moral Ideology." In R*eview of Child Development and Personality,* vol. 1, edited by M. L. Hoffman and L. W. Hoffman. New York: Russell Sage, 1964.

Kurshan, Neil. *Raising Your Child to Be a Mensch.* New York: Atheneum, 1987.

LeShan, Eda. *The Parent's Guide to Everyday Problems.* New York: Scholastic Four Winds, 1981.

Lickona, Thomas. *Raising Good Children.* New York: Bantam Books, 1983.

Marston, Stephanie. *The Magic of Encouragement*. New York: Pocket Books, 1990.

Nelson, Jane. *Positive Discipline*. Fair Oaks, Calif.: Sunrise Press, 1981.

Oppenheim, Joanne, Boegehold, Betty, and Brenner, Barbara. *Raising a Confident Child*. New York: Pantheon Books, 1984.

Peairs, Lillian, and Peairs, Richard H. *What Every Child Needs*. New York: Harper and Row, 1974.

Piaget, Jean. *The Moral Judgment of the Child*. New York: The Free Press, 1965.

Riley, Sue Spayth. *How to Generate Values in Young Children*. Washington, D.C.: National Association for the Education of Young Children, 1984.

Rosenthal, R., and Jacobson, L. *Pygmalion in the Classroom*. New York: Holt, Rinehart, and Winston, 1968.

Schulman, Michael, and Mekler, Eva. *Bringing Up a Moral Child*. Reading, Mass: Addison-Wesley, 1985.

Segal, Julius, and Yahraes, Herbert. *A Child's Journey*. New York: McGraw-Hill, 1978.

Shiff, Eileen, Ed. *Experts Advise Parents*. New York: Delta Books, 1987.

Simon, Sidney. *I Am Lovable and Capable*. Niles, Ill.: Argus Communications, 1973.

Staub, Ervin. *Positive Social Behavior and Morality*, vol. 2. New York: Academic Press, 1979.

Wyckoff, Jerry L., and Unell, Barbara. *How to Discipline Your Six to Twelve Year Old . . . Without Losing Your Mind*. New York: Doubleday, 1991.

York, Phyllis, York, David, and Wachtel, Ted. *Toughlove Solutions*. New York: Bantam Books, 1985.

Ziglar, Zig. *Raising Positive Kids in a Negative World*. New York: Ballantine Books, 1985.

Index